LOVE ME passionately . . .
LOVE ME tenderly . . .

LOVE ME passionately . . .
LOVE ME tenderly . . .

A journey into the love of God

Paul F Taylor

authorHOUSE®

AuthorHouse™
1663 Liberty Drive
Bloomington, IN 47403
www.authorhouse.com
Phone: 1-800-839-8640

First published by AuthorHouse   11/07/2011

ISBN: 978-1-4670-1392-5 (sc)

Printed in the United States of America

Any people depicted in stock imagery provided by Thinkstock are models, and such images are being used for illustrative purposes only.
Certain stock imagery © Thinkstock.

This book is printed on acid-free paper.

Front cover from an original oil painting by Yvonne Lee. Used by permission.
Scripture taken from the New Kings James Version. Copyright © 1982 by Thomas Nelson, Inc. Used by permission. All rights reserved.
Scripture taken from the HOLY BIBLE, NEW INTERNATIONAL VERSION®. Copyright © 1973, 1978, 1984 International Bible Society. Used by permission of Zondervan. All rights reserved.
The "NIV" and "New International Version" trademarks are registered in the United States Patent and Trademark Office by International Bible Society. Use of either trademark requires the permission of International Bible Society.

INDEX

ACKNOWLEDGEMENTS

To my wife, Moira, whose inspiration and encouragement made this book possible. Without her enthusiasm, my studies would not have been printed in a book form as you now have. She has been such a blessing to me.

ABOUT THE AUTHOR

"We've trained you to think logically," the professor told Paul after he had obtained a degree in maths at Hull University. Soon after, while working as a systems analyst in the computer department of a large national firm, God spoke to him.

He then turned his back on rosy money making prospects and went to the Elim Bible College, which was then in Capel, Surrey. Here he found that his logical thinking did not help him understand such things as the love of God. So he spent time studying to get to know more about God, and praying to get to know Him personally.

After leaving Bible College, he was the pastor of Elim Churches in Banbridge, Northern Ireland, Monaghan in Eire, and in Woolwich near London. But it was when he was the pastor of the Elim church in Nuneaton that his teaching ministry began to blossom.

While in Nuneaton, his wife, Moira, and he believed that the Lord was leading them out of pastoring churches and was challenging them to trust Him to reveal how He wanted them to serve Him. They moved to Swadlincote, near Burton-on-Trent; where they spent time seeking God.

They started a ministry called Kingdom Lifestyle ministries, where their aim was to come alongside local churches to help them and to reach out into the community. As part of this ministry, Paul started Bible Studies which really blessed others. So he decided to put them into book form to make them available to others who would benefit from them.

The studies are different to any others that he had done. As he continued to seek God, a deeper intimacy developed between the Lord and him. This relationship is reflected in the studies. They encourage people to seek God and have a more loving and intimate relationship with Him.

Moira and Paul are in fellowship at St John's Church of England in Newhall, where Paul has been a member of the Parochial Church Council (PCC).

PREFACE

I have always enjoyed preparing and presenting Bible Studies and the congregation has always received them with enthusiasm.

Some people joined the church because of them.
Some taped them and sent them to their friends in other countries.
Recently, one person quoted from some studies I did well over 20 years ago.

However, one short series I did was most enthusiastically received.

It comprised a series of quotes from the Bible developing the theme of reasons why we should praise God. In turn, each person read a quote aloud. The presence of God increased as the study progressed. There were more positive comments about those studies than any other I have done.

Every time I repeated these studies, the results were the same. What I did not realize then was that God was showing me a new way of presenting a Bible Study.

Developing this style, I presented some Bible studies to some friends who really enjoyed them and were greatly blessed.

So, I decided to put these studies into a book which is written in a style that will involve the reader. The studies were prayerfully prepared to help people receive the Word of God into their lives and develop a greater intimate relationship with the Lord.

INTRODUCTION

This book is different.

It is not a study book about the 23rd Psalm.

It is not a book about the Shepherd of the Psalm.

It is about responding to the love of the Shepherd of the Psalm, and getting to know Him better.

With the help of The Holy Spirit, this book will take you on a journey through the Psalm into the presence of the Lord, the Good Shepherd.

As each verse unfolds, the word will give you a personal and intimate revelation of a loving and compassionate Heavenly Father.

As you go through each chapter, you will find the book helping . . .

- ➤ To encourage you to meditate on the Word of God, to confess the Word and to do it. (Joshua 1:8.)

- ➤ To increase your faith in the Lord. (Romans 10:8-9, 17.) You will be encouraged to put your entire life into His hands, and to trust Him for all things.

- ➤ To inspire you to spend more time in His presence. There you will get to know Him and be able to develop your fellowship with Him.

➢ To bring you into a more intimate relationship with Jesus. (Revelation 2:4-5.)

And you will begin to soar with Him as on wings like eagles. (Isaiah 40:31.)

How To Use This Book

The most important thing is to ask the Holy Spirit to inspire you and to implant the truth into your heart. He will guide you into all truth and will make the truth come alive to you. He will reveal Jesus to you. If you do not ask the Holy Spirit for help, the book will be just words and will not profit you.

Each chapter has two parts.

Paragraphs in italics are either comments to guide you through the study, or small portions of study to help you understand the truth in the chapter.

The other paragraphs are to be confessed aloud. These are confessions of faith.

This book can be studied alone, or in a small group.
Take your time as you read each paragraph.
Pause between each one; give the Holy Spirit the opportunity to minister to you.

If you are in a group, each person in turn reads one paragraph. The leader can read the *italic paragraphs.* At the end of each chapter, allow time for anyone to share briefly any truths that ministered to them, or blessed them.

The scripture references in brackets after the confessions do not need to be read out. They are there for you to look them up if you so desire. They will confirm the truth of what you have spoken, or direct you in further study.

Then, whether you are in a group or on your own, have a time of thanksgiving and worship to the Lord about these truths.

Do not rush.

Do one chapter a week.

It is important to have the Holy Spirit write the Word on your heart and become part of your life. So, here are some suggestions to help you.

a)   Before you start the chapter, ask the Holy Spirit to help you.

b). You can repeat each chapter in that week.

c). It will bless you to go to sleep with some of these truths on your mind, and it will bless you to confess them first thing in the morning—as it has blessed me.

Read this book with your heart

not your head.

CHAPTER 1

MY LOVING SHEPHERD

The LORD is my shepherd; I shall not want. (Psalm 23:1 NKJV.)

*The words "The Lord is my shepherd" comes from Hebrew words which are one of the names of God. A name of God describes His unchanging character and nature. It tells us what God is and what He always will do. Therefore, God is a shepherd because it is His nature to be a shepherd. He cannot cease to be a shepherd because it is part of His unchanging character to be a shepherd. He will always do those things a shepherd would do because He cannot do anything else. We can say that "The Lord is **my** shepherd" if we belong to His flock.*

Jesus came to seek and save the lost, like a shepherd seeking his lost sheep.

I thank You Jesus because as my Shepherd You sought me out when I was lost, You brought me to Yourself and You will look after me. (Ezekiel 34:11-12; Luke 19:10.)

I thank You Jesus that as I accepted Your call to come to You, and turned from my sin, You are now my Shepherd. You know my name. You know me. You know all about me. I have a personal relationship with You. (John 10:3, 14; Luke 15:4-7.)

I thank You Jesus because You are my Good Shepherd. And because You are my Shepherd, You talk to me in such a way that I can hear Your voice. I listen to You and I will follow You. (John 10:4, 16, 27.)

As my Shepherd, Jesus loves me.

I thank You Jesus because You are my Good Shepherd You love me so much that You laid down Your life for me. (John 10:11.)

I thank You Lord, that You are my Shepherd whose love for me is so unquestionably immeasurable that You hold me firmly close to Your heart . . . securely close . . . snugly close . . . You will always look after me, You will continually guide me, You will constantly lead me and You will forever hold me in a loving intimate embrace. (Isaiah 40:10-11.)

The phrase "the apple of the eye" refers to the pupil. This is the most precious part of the eye, which is why the eyelids immediately protect it when there is even the suggestion of danger. "The apple of the eye" refers to that which is ardently loved, passionately cared for, extremely precious, and zealously protected.

I thank You Lord that You are my Shepherd and in Your sight I am the apple of Your eye, extremely precious and passionately loved. You will enthusiastically care for me and look after me, You will fervently help me, You will earnestly protect me, You will jealously guard and keep me. (Deuteronomy 32:10; Psalm 17:8.)

As my Shepherd, Jesus will never forget me, nor leave me, nor let me go.

I thank You Lord that You are my Shepherd who loves me, and therefore there will never be a moment You will forget me, for You have engraved my name on the palm of Your hands, and it is there for You always to see. (Isaiah 49:15-16.)

I thank You Lord that You are my Shepherd who thinks the world of me. You will always be at my side, continually holding me in Your hand and will let no one take me away from You. Continually underneath me are your everlasting arms, always supporting me, constantly holding me, incessantly carrying me. (John 10:28-29; Deuteronomy 33:27.)

I thank You Lord that You are my Shepherd who cares for me so much that You will never leave me nor forsake me. It doesn't matter what mood I am in, it doesn't matter what I feel like, it doesn't matter what situation I am in, You are always there at my side. (Hebrews 13:5.)

The Lord will never change; He will always be my Shepherd.

I thank You Lord that because You do not change, You will always be my Shepherd and You will always be there for me, You will always be at my side. (Malachi 3:6.)

I thank You Jesus that You are the same yesterday, today, and forever. You change not, and You will always continue to be my Good Shepherd, yesterday, today, tomorrow, next week, next year . . . forever and forever. (Hebrews 13:8.)

As my Shepherd, He will always care for me.

I thank You Lord that You are my Shepherd and as I am precious to You, You will continue to watch over me, keeping me from all harm. Wherever I go, whatever I do, whatever situation I am in, whatever the future has in store for me, You will always watch over me and You will continue to bless me. (Psalm 121:5-8; Genesis 48:15-16 NIV.)

I thank You Lord that You are my Shepherd and as You are my Shepherd, You care for me affectionately and watchfully. I can cast all my cares, worries and concerns upon You. You will sustain me. (Psalm 55:22; 95:7; 1 Peter 5:7.)

I thank You Lord that because You are my Shepherd You have to look after me. You have to protect me, You must guide me, You are obliged to comfort me and You are compelled to provide for me. (John 10:4, 28-29; Psalm 23:1, 4.)

I thank You Lord that You are my Shepherd therefore You are my comforter. You will comfort me in all of my troubles. You will comfort me when I am downcast. You will reassure me when I am lonely, You will calm me when I am anxious, You will set my mind at rest when I am worried, You will strengthen me when I am weak. (Psalm 23:4; 2 Corinthians 1:3-4; 7:6.)

I thank You Lord, that You chose me to be a member of Your flock. I did not choose You but You chose me and wanted to be my Shepherd. And as I accepted Your call and came to You, You received me into Your flock and became my Shepherd. And I thank You that as You chose to be my Shepherd You will always be my Shepherd, for You cannot "uncommit" Yourself to me, You cannot change Your mind and decide to turn me away. You will always be my Shepherd; You will always care for me. (John 6:37; 15:16.)

Because the Lord is my Shepherd, I shall not want.

This can mean two things—

Firstly, "I shall not want" because my Good Shepherd is all I need, He is my life; He is my everything. I do not need to find anything else for my satisfaction. I do not need anyone else to give me fulfilment of life and purpose. How can I be discontent when I have the ever present, all-powerful, continually gracious Lord at my side?

Secondly, "I shall not want" because God will meet all of my needs. Because my Good Shepherd cares for me He will always look after me, He will always look over me, and He will always make provision for me. How can I be in want if I have a loving good and wise shepherd who is willing and able to provide for me?

Lord, I thank You that You have promised to answer my prayers. Indeed Lord, You care for me so much that You know all about me. You know all about my life. You know what I need even before I ask You. Lord how wonderful You are. (John 16:23-24; Matthew 6:8.)

I thank You Jesus that You have promised to give me Your peace in times of troubles and trials. It is a peace that surpasses all knowledge and understanding. It is a peace that will keep me from worry and anxiety in times of distress. (John 14:27; 16:33; Philippians 4:7.)

I thank You Lord for You have promised to give me Your joy. It is a joy that is full. Even when I go through trials and testings, I will experience Your joy that is glorious and victorious. It is such a great and exuberant joy that I will be unable to put my feelings into words. Jesus, You will fill me with Your joy, in its entire fullness, and it will saturate so much my entire being, that I will not be able to contain it. O Lord, how great You are. (John 15:11; 17:13; 1 Peter 1:6-8.)

Lord, I thank You that You have promised that if I seek You first, if I follow You and live a life that pleases You, then all the things in life that I need You will supply. Be it food or clothing of life or health—You will do this because You love me and I am precious to You. You will do this because You are my Shepherd, who will look after His sheep, and I am following You. (Matthew 6:25-33.)

I thank You Lord, that You have promised to give me strength in times of weakness, provision in times of need, comfort in times of sorrow, hope in times of despair, blessing and glory in times of persecution, joy in times of difficulty, peace in times of worry . . . O Lord, how great You are, how wonderful, how marvellous You are to me. I worship You, I adore You, and I praise Your wonderful Name. (Isaiah 40:29-31; 61:1-3; Matthew 6:8-11; 1 Peter 4:14.)

Father, I thank You that as I fear, honour and worship You, I will lack nothing. I thank You Lord that as I seek You, I will lack no good thing. Indeed Lord, as we walk together You will not withhold any good thing from me. God how wonderful You are. You did not spare Your Beloved Son, Jesus, but gave Him up to die on the cross for me—since You did not spare Your Son, how much more will You also along with Him, graciously give me all things. (Psalm 34:9-10; 84:11; Romans 8:32.)

Lord, You are everything to me; You are so lovely, so wonderful that I will not find such an amazing love anywhere else. I need not go anywhere else to find life. For You are my joy, You are my peace; You alone give me satisfaction, fulfilment and purpose. You are my Good Shepherd, I shall not lack anything; I shall not want, for You are all I need. I worship You, I adore You, I love You Lord.

Because I belong to You, Lord God, and You are my Shepherd . . .

. . . I will shout for joy to You, O Lord . . .

. . . I will worship You, O Lord, with gladness . . .

. . . I will come before You with joyful songs . . .

. . . I will enter Your gates with thanksgiving and Your courts with praise . . .

. . . I will give thanks to You, O Lord, and praise Your Name . . .

. . . I will do this to You, O Lord, for You are good to me and Your love for me will endure forever; You will be faithful to me through all generations. (Psalm 100.)

CHAPTER 2

THE OASIS OF LOVE

He makes me to lie down in green pastures; He leads me beside the still waters. (Psalm 23:2 NKJV.)

He leads His flock into a place, where there is an abundance of young, luxurious grass and loads of watering places. It is like an oasis—a thriving and flourishing spot in the middle of a desert. It is a place of rest and refreshment, where there is shelter from the scorching sun. It is a place of refuge from any prowling predators. The flock, surrounded by abundance, and, having satisfied their wants, are lying down amidst this extravagance and security, with calm contentment. It is not merely a flock enjoying rest; it is a flock whose needs are supplied. They are lying down satisfied, in the midst of abundant supplies. There is the sense of calmness and peace, rest and tranquillity, safety and security. They know that their Shepherd is with them and that all is well. They need not go anywhere else. They have all they need here.

He makes me to lie down in green pastures.

I thank You Lord that You bring me into Your "Oasis of Love". There You cause me to lie down in pastures of fresh and tender grass, where I can lie at ease and be content. In Your oasis, I will find rest and refreshment.

Lord, I thank You that in this oasis, I can relax with You. I will be calm and content. For I know that I will be secure and safe. No one can make

7

me afraid. Nothing can cause me ill harm, for You are at my side, looking over me, looking after me. (Isaiah 14:30; 17:2; Zephaniah 3:13.)

I thank You Lord that You seek out and find the sheep that are lost. You love and care for them so much that You bring them back to Your oasis. You bind up the injured. You strengthen the weak. Lord, this oasis is a haven of rest, it is a shelter from the storms of life, it is like "heaven on earth," for I am in Your presence and I desire to be nowhere else. (Jeremiah 33:12-13; Zephaniah 2:7; Ezekiel 34:14-16.)

I thank You Jesus, my Good Shepherd that You are always with me and You are always at my side. I thank You that there is no need for me to look anywhere else for my needs. I thank You that there is no need to wander to find some other source to find satisfaction, for being with You is life itself.

Lord, I thank You that when I am burdened with trials and heavy laden with problems I can come to You, and You will give me rest. You have invited me to come, and You will never turn me away. You will never let me down. You will always be my refuge, my help, and my strength. (Matthew 11:28-29.)

The Hebrew words for "green pastures" refer to "tender grass"; the first shoots of vegetation from the earth. This is young herbage, fresh grass and is delicate food. The Hebrew words are different from those that describe ripe grass that is ready for mowing, or is food for cattle or horses. (1 Kings 18:5.) The green pasture He puts us in is just what we need, delicious, satisfying and fulfilling.

Lord, the pasture you will feed me on is good pasture. It is abundant and pleasing, delicious and delightful, bringing much pleasure and satisfaction. The pasture is rich being excellent and nutritious, and will make me strong and healthy. (Ezekiel 34:14.)

Jesus, I thank You that You are my Good Shepherd, who loves me so much that You laid down Your life for me. You will lead me. You will guide me. You will go ahead of me and bring me into those green pastures, where I will find joy, rest, contentment and abundant life. You will give me a life that is superabundant in quantity, superior in quality, excessive in every way. (John 10:3-4, 9-11.)

The green pastures speak of the Word of God. For we do not live on bread alone, but upon every word that comes out from the mouth of God. (Matthew 4:4.)

Lord, I thank You that Your Word is like milk to the young converts to nourish them and cause them to grow and develop. It is like meat to Your older ones that will help them mature and be strong. (Hebrews 5:11-14.)

Lord, I thank You for Your Word. I receive Your Word with enthusiasm and delight as if it was the choicest of all foods. Your Word gives me great joy and causes my heart to rejoice. (Jeremiah 15:16.)

Lord, Your Word is very precious to me. It is of greater value than gold, even far more precious than pure gold. It is sweeter than honey—yes even sweeter and richer than the dripping honey tasted straight from the honeycomb. Your Word gives me great pleasure and in keeping Your Word, there is great reward. (Psalm 19:10-11.)

I talked to a farmer in Ireland about the Word of God and the need for us to take time in feeding from it. He told me something about farm life. Sometimes he would just stand and closely watch his cattle eating the grass and chewing the cud. He would count the number of times that the cow chewed—one . . . two . . . three . . . twenty . . . thirty . . . thirty-seven . . . If the cow reached about thirty-seven, then the farmer was content. He knew that the cow was chewing the cud thoroughly and as she properly digested the grass, she would receive full benefit from it. If however, the count only reached six or seven, then he would call in the vet, for there would be something wrong with the cow, since she was not chewing the cud properly, and would receive no benefit from the undigested grass. Every time he called the vet out on this basis, the vet always found that there was something wrong with the cow. So with us—if we do not spend time digesting the word of God through prayer, reading and studying, then there is something wrong with our spiritual life and we need to seek God to get the problem put right.

Lord, I love Your Word and take great delight in it. Your Word will revive my soul, it will give joy to my heart, it will make me wise, it will instruct me, it will direct me, it will warn me. Help me to keep Your Word Lord, for in this there is great reward. (Psalm 19:7-11; 119:47-48.)

Oh Lord, I do love Your Word. I think about it all day long. I continually ponder on Your Word. I keep it in my mind and my heart that I might not sin against You—for I love You Lord, and I do want to please You in my thoughts, words, and actions. (Psalm 119:11, 97.)

Lord, to me Your Word is extremely precious, far more precious than anything else in this world. Lord, help me to keep it in my mind and meditate on it. Help me to keep it in my heart, so that it inspires and directs my life. Help me to keep it and confess it, for I know that in doing these things You will cause me to flourish and have success in all I do. (Psalm 119:72; Joshua 1:7-8.)

He leads me beside the still waters.

The "still waters" are waters of quietness. They are not violent torrents, which would terrify the sheep with their roar, and sweep them away with the current. But these waters are gently flowing, where a wonderful and satisfying rest is enjoyed.

I remember watching the River Bann in Ireland. At its source was a dam, which not only held the water back to provide a reservoir, but it also controlled the flow of the water. Consequently, the river flowed in a gentle and peaceful way. It provided a source of water to the sheep that grazed in adjacent fields. One autumn, there were several torrential downpours. The dam was so full that it was unable to control the water flow. This transformed the river from a gentle flow to a rushing torrent. There was no way that any sheep could drink from this river now. Then I saw a sheep carcass flowing down. The raging river had somehow snatched the sheep from its bank and dragged it to its death. So, Our Shepherd brings us beside those still waters. From these waters we can drink safely and securely, knowing they are there for our benefit. These waters will quench our every thirst.

Lord—I long after joy, pleasure and happiness. Only in Your presence have I found fullness of joy, a joy that is so full that I cannot express what I feel like. In Your presence, there is unlimited, inexhaustible, happiness—pleasures forevermore. For as I come to You, You will give me living water, which will not only quench my thirst, but it will be like a spring of water in me that incessantly wells up and gives me eternal and everlasting life. (Psalm 16:11; 1 Peter 1:8; John 4:10-14.)

Lord, in this world of turmoil and uncertainty, I just want to know peace. As I come to You, You will give me what I desire; a peace in the middle of trouble and trials; a peace that will remain through all uncertainties; a peace that will overwhelm all fears; a peace that will keep me calm in all situations; a peace that will guard my heart and mind. You give me a perfect peace that I desire, one that will not go away as I stay close to You. Lord, I praise You, for You are so wonderful. (John 14:27; 16:33; Philippians 4:7; Isaiah 26:3.)

Lord, I desire to know the purpose of my life and the reason for my existence. I thank You Lord that as I am so important to You, You have got thoughts and plans for me, thoughts for my welfare, plans for my peace, thoughts and plans that will give me hope and a future, and will cause me to prosper. You created plans for me before I was born. You already have plans for me to walk in and works for me to do. As I seek You Lord, lead me in those ways that will glorify Your Name. (Jeremiah 29:11; Psalm 139:16; Ephesians 2:10.)

As the deer earnestly longs for and desperately desires streams of water, so my heart eagerly craves after You, my soul fervently yearns for You. For I just want to be with You, I long to be in Your presence. You will quench my every thirst—and I will never thirst again. You will give me life, abundant life, a life that is full and overflowing with blessing, where there will be a superabundance of joy, peace and love. And I will be more than satisfied in all areas of my life. Thanks be to You Lord, who gives good things without measure and without limit. (Psalm 42:1-2; John 4:14; 10:10.)

Lord, I thank You that I can come to You and drink, and You will not only quench my thirst, but You will fill me up so much that from out of my inner most being will flow rivers of living water. (John 7:37-39.)

Lord, I thank You that You are my Good Shepherd. You will bring me into Your "Oasis of Love". You will cause me to lie down in green pastures. You will lead me beside the still waters. As I come to You I will never hunger. As I trust You and rely upon You, I will never thirst again. Lord, You are so gracious and loving—to think that You care so much for me. Lord, I worship and adore You, singing praises to Your wonderful Name. (John 6:35.)

CHAPTER 3

HE LOVINGLY RESTORES MY SOUL

He restores my soul. (Psalm 23:3 NKJV.)

I thank You Jesus that You are the Shepherd and "Overseer" of my soul. You look over me continually with Your love. You see everything that is going on in my life. I am so important to You that there is never a moment when You do not care for me and You are not looking after me. (1 Peter 2:25.)

Lord I thank You that I can rest contentedly knowing that You know all about me every moment of every day. You always know my needs and desires, my hurts and my pains. You always know when I am in anguish or despair. You never miss hearing any sigh that comes from my heart. You do not miss seeing any of my tears.

Lord, I thank You that as my Good Shepherd, You will bring me to Your "Oasis of Love". You will make me sit down in the green pasture. You will lead me by the still water. You will restore my soul.

To restore means to make good the damage, to set something to right. It means to build something up again and to bring it back to the original state. When some buildings at the Windsor Castle were burnt by fire, many items were damaged, and the beautiful architecture of the building was ruined. However, many craftsmen came together and worked hard and long to restore the building and its content back to its former glory. It almost looks as if the fire did not happen.

To restore means to bring someone back to health, returning their strength and vigour. To restore the soul means to bring it back to the place where it should be so that life returns. The soul will be mended, rebuilt and made whole. It will be refreshed, quickened and brought back to fullness of life. Our All-Sufficient Shepherd knows what we need and He restores and revives our soul.

I thank You Jesus that when I am tired and weary, I can come to You for help. When I feel so weak and helpless I can trust You. When I am so worn out, that I can't do anything myself, I can wait upon You. For You will increase my power when I am weak, worn down and worn out. You will renew my strength. You will cause me to soar on wings like eagles. Then I will run and not grow weary, I will walk and not faint. (Isaiah 40:29-31.)

I thank You Jesus that when I am exhausted, or worn down with worry or burdens, I can come to You and You will give me rest. I thank You Lord that when I am worried, troubled or anxious, when everything seems to be so helpless and hopeless, I can come to You and You will calm my fears, You will give me peace, You will refresh my soul. (Matthew 11:28-29.)

Lord, there are those times when situations happen that cause my heart to break and make me despair. But Lord, I thank You that You are still at my side. You know what I am going through. Because You care for me You will help me, You will comfort me, You will pour into me Your love and peace. You will bind me up and restore my soul. (Isaiah 61:1.)

Lord, I thank You that when I mourn You are at my side and You will comfort me. You will strengthen and bless me. When I grieve You will anoint me with the oil of gladness and make me smile again. When I am in despair, You will take away the garment of heaviness and put upon me the garment of praise. Lord, You are my comforter, You are my helper. You are the restorer of my soul. (Isaiah 61:1-3.)

Solomon wrote, "Like the cold of snow in time of harvest is a faithful messenger to those who send him, for he refreshes the soul of his masters." (Proverbs 25:13

NKJV). The snow in time of harvest does not refer to a shower of snow or hail, which would be terrifying and harmful rather than refreshing. In Solomon's days the mountain snow would be stored in a cold cleft of a rock. So in the summer scorching heat, when the drinks would be warm and unappetising, the snow would be brought and placed into the drink to make it more refreshing and appetising to the thirsty. This is similar to when we place ice cubes in our drinks. However, this refreshment was for the physical body and would only last a short time. This is why Solomon said that even though this was refreshing, yet more reviving than the iced drink was the faithful messenger who would bring a message of comfort or encouragement. For this would touch a person's soul and revive it. So Jesus, our Shepherd, the Good Shepherd, the Great Shepherd, the Overseer of our Souls, comes to us to give us comfort and encouragement to our hearts and He will refresh and restore our souls.

Lord, sometimes I get so exhausted and tired that I can hardly move a muscle to lift a hand. Yet Lord, You know all about this, and You will send Your Holy Spirit to move upon me to refresh me and give me rest and strength.

Lord, sometimes there are situations that hurt me and cause me anguish. It is all about other people's actions, decisions or situations. I can't do anything about it. Yet You care for me. You will come along side me. You will put Your arms around me and comfort me and give me Your peace.

Lord, there are times when I make a mistake. I am not happy about it—and I don't feel too good about myself. But God, You are my Father and You do not stop loving me, even if I have slipped up. For I am Your child and You still love me, regardless of my mistakes and shortcomings. And Jesus, You are my Shepherd and You will come to me and bless me. You will reaffirm Your love to me and revive my soul.

Lord, I thank You that when I feel down and out, You know that I need a touch from You. You know when I am dispirited and in need. You love me and care for me. You will bless me and make me aware that You are at my side, that You are with me and that You are holding me securely in Your hand.

There was a time when I needed to use the flashgun for my camera, but I hadn't used it for some time. I picked it up, placed it upon the camera, and switched it on. It did not work. The batteries were flat and needed recharging. They were put in the battery charger, and soon I was taking photographs with the flashgun. This is a picture of what our soul is like if we are not in contact with God. We are flat and miserable. There is not much life in us—if any! We need to be recharged, or restored, and that can only be done when we are in contact or communion with the Lord. However, the parallel with the battery ends there. The battery can hold its charge for some time before it needs recharging. We cannot keep our life at all; we can do this only when we are in constant and continual communion with God.

Lord, I thank You so much that You love me dearly. I am very precious to You. I thank You that You enjoy being with me. You take great delight in my company. Therefore You will help me stay in fellowship with You. You will encourage me to spend time with You, so that our relationship will develop and deepen. (Revelation 3:20.)

I thank You Lord for Your Word. It keeps me pure. It builds me up. When I read Your Word, it will revive my soul and bring joy to my heart. (Psalm 19:7-8 NIV; Psalm 119:9-11; Hebrews 5:12-14.)

Lord, You are like a vine, and I am one of Your branches. As the sap flows through the vine to the branches causing the branches to live and produce fruit, so Lord as I remain connected to You—in fellowship with You—Your life will flow into me and I will live. Lord, help me to remain in communion with You, so that Your life, Your joy, Your love, Your peace will flow into me and cause me to live and produce fruit. (John 15:1-5.)

I thank You Lord that when I have sinned, if I confess and turn from my sin, You will rejoice, for You just want to have fellowship with me again. So You will forgive me and cleanse me from all unrighteousness, You will come to my side so that we will enjoy being with each other, and we will walk together again. (Luke 15:10; 1 John 1:7-9.)

I thank You Lord that when I am backslidden, I can repent and return to You. You are so gracious and forgiving, that You will forgive me, You will renew me and cleanse me. You will restore to me the joy of Your salvation and I will again know the fellowship of Your Holy Spirit. (Psalm 51:3, 8-12.)

There are those days when I am brooding upon my setbacks and circumstances, not knowing what to think, wondering what to do, what is going to happen—then You come to me, You comfort me and fill me with Your peace, and You revive my soul. O Lord, how lovely You are. There is no one like You.

There are those times when I am inwardly crying or in despair, and wonder what is going to happen next—then You come to me and breathe Your life into me, giving me hope and strength. You come to me and suddenly I am made whole. You do it quietly and graciously, gently and lovingly. I lift up my heart to You in thanksgiving and worship, and in tears, I am lost in love, wonder and praise.

Lord, You are my Good Shepherd, constantly watching over me, knowing all about me, every moment of every day. You bring me into Your "Oasis of Love". You make me lie down in green pastures. You lead me beside still waters. You restore my soul. Such is Your love for me, and I love You.

CHAPTER 4

HE TENDERLY LEADS

He leads me beside the still waters . . . He leads me in the paths of righteousness. (Psalm 23:2-3 NKJV.)

To know that God leads and guides us is so wonderful, and twice in this Psalm, David rejoices in this truth. In verse two, David says that God leads us beside the still waters. The Hebrew word used here mainly means to lead with great care and compassion, emphasizing a shepherd's loving concern for his flock as he leads them to places of rest and refreshment. In verse three, David says that God will lead them in the paths of righteousness. The Hebrew word used here mainly means to lead in the right path or in the correct direction.

A guide is a person who shows the way, especially to people who do not know it or who are strangers to the area. He will direct them to the places that they are interested in, and will warn them of the places where they would do well to avoid.

Sheep are animals who are totally dependent upon their shepherd. On their own, they wander where they want to go; they do not know where to go for food or drink; they are vulnerable to any predator and exposed to dangers. God compares us to sheep that have gone astray, gone their own way, and followed their own desires and pleasures; sheep who need a shepherd. (Isaiah 53:6; Ezekiel 34:5; Matthew 9:36.)

The Lord is my guide because He loves me.

Jesus, You are my Good Shepherd who loved me so much that You laid down Your life for me. I am very special to You because You know my name. Therefore, You will lead me by going ahead of me, and You will call me by my name encouraging me to follow You. By leading me, You are showing the way to go and making sure that the way is safe. (John 10:3-4, 11, 27.)

I thank You Father that You tend me like a shepherd. When I am frail, You will take me in Your arms and carry me close to Your heart. You will pay loving attention to me, and when I go through difficult times, You will tenderly guide me as a shepherd would gently lead those who have young. (Isaiah 40:11.)

Lord, I thank You that You will lead me according to Your unfailing love and constant mercy. When I am weak, You will not leave me behind, nor show no interest in me, but You will take me by the hand and keep me. You will guide me by Your strength and power. You will lead me into the place where You dwell, Your "Oasis of Love", where I will find rest and refreshment. (Exodus 15:13; Isaiah 42:6.)

I praise You Lord, I am so precious to You. Therefore, You will always be with me. I thank You Lord that You love me so much that You will take great delight in me, You will rejoice over me, and You will lead me with great joy. (Isaiah 43:4-5; 55:12; 62:4-5.)

He is a good guide because He knows what is best for me.

I thank You Lord that Your ways are supremely greater than my ways; Your thoughts are far superior to my thoughts. You will lead me according to Your counsel and wisdom. You will teach me what is best for me, and what things are for my profit and welfare. You will direct me and lead me in the way that I should go. I know that I can trust You for You care for me. (Isaiah 55:8-9; Psalm 73:24; Isaiah 48:17.)

I thank You Lord that You will teach me in the way that I should go. When I have to make a decision, You will instruct me in the path I am to take. You will counsel me; You will guide me; You will always be watching over me. As I submit myself to You, You will guide me in the right and just way. As I follow You, You will teach me Your way. O Lord, How great You are. How good You are to me. (Psalm 32:8; 25:9.)

He is a good guide because He knows the way I should go.

I thank You Father that You will always guide me in the way that You want me to go, for You know what is best for me. For if I turn to the left or the right, straying from the right path, then I will hear You saying, "This is the way, walk in it." (Isaiah 30:21.)

I thank You Father for when I go through a difficult situation, and I struggle not knowing which way to go, You will lead me, You will guide me as if I was going through a desert, and You will guide me safely so that I need not fear about anything. (Psalms 78:52-53.)

He is a good guide because He knows what is going to happen tomorrow.

Lord, I thank You that You know the end from the beginning, You know what is still to come; You know what is going to happen. I thank You that You tell me not to worry about what will happen tomorrow. So, Lord, You will lead and guide me according to Your wisdom and knowledge, and I can totally trust You. I thank You Lord that You will prepare me today for tomorrow, so that when tomorrow comes, I will be ready for the problems and difficulties that will come. (Isaiah 42:9; 46:9-10; John 13:19; Matthew 6:33-34.)

I thank You Lord that You have plans and purposes for my life. You have thoughts for my peace and welfare. You have plans to give me hope and a future. You have works for me to do that You have already planned for me to walk in. Lord, I thank You that I can put my life into Your hands, and You will guide me. (Jeremiah 29:11; Ephesians 2:10.)

Lord, I thank You that You will always be my guide. Wherever I am, whatever situation I am in You will continually guide me. You always know where the "Oasis of Love" is. You know where the green pastures and still waters are. You will guide me to them. (Isaiah 58:11.)

Lord, You are my God forever and ever, and ever and ever. You will be my guide for every single day of my life. Lord, I just put my hands into Your hands. I submit my life to You and You will lead the way. (Psalm 48:14; 139:10.)

How God leads us.

God can lead us in several ways. Here are four examples.

Lord, I thank You that You can lead me through Your Word. For Your Word is like a lamp to my feet—so that even on a dark night it will show me the way, preventing me from tripping over obstacles, or straying into danger. Your Word is like a light to my path, so that I can clearly see the way that I am going. (Psalm 119:105.)

Lord, I thank You that Your Holy Spirit will prompt me which way to go. I will submit to His influence and control over my life. He will bear witness with me as to what I should not do and which way I should not go. He will lead me, He will guide me, He will show me the way. (Romans 8:14; Matthew 4:1; Psalm 143:10.)

Lord, I thank You that You will lead me by Your peace and joy that is in me. For when I lose Your peace, I know that I have gone the wrong way or done something wrong. I thank You Lord that You give me the opportunity of correcting the wrong, or going back to that place when I last knew Your joy. As I trust You, You will fill me with Your joy and peace. (Colossians 3:15; Romans 14:17; 15:13; Isaiah 55:12.)

Lord I thank You that there will be those times when You will speak to me. You will lead me and call me to follow. And I will listen to Your voice, I will recognise it and I will obey and follow. Lord, I thank You that You know my name, and You will call me by my name, and I will follow You. (John 10:3-4, 16.)

Lord, help me to stay close by Your side and develop an intimate relationship with You, then I will be sensitive to the promptings of Your peace, joy and of Your Holy Spirit. Then I will recognise Your voice and know when You are speaking to me. Lord, I love You, stay close to me, hold me close to Your side, embrace me tight in Your arms.

Sometimes God leads us in mysterious ways. The hymn writer William Cowper lived from 1731 to 1800. Sometimes he suffered great mental anguish and occasionally he would consider committing suicide. On one such night, he hailed a horse driven cab to take him to the River Thames. He had planned to throw himself into the river to drown. However, a thick fog carpeted London, and the driver of the cab lost his way. Cowper ran out of patience. Determined to get to the Thames, he told the cab to stop and he leapt from it. Stumbling through the fog, he got lost, and after a while, he was amazed to find that he was back at his own home! He fell to his knees in praise to God and thanked Him for the fog that had stopped him from killing himself. Knowing that God had allowed the fog to come to save him, Cowper wrote the words of this hymn:

God moves in a mysterious way
His wonders to perform;
He plants His footsteps in the sea,
And rides upon the storm.

You fearful saints, fresh courage take;
The clouds you so much dread
Are big with mercy, and will break
In blessing on your head!

I thank You Lord that You do guide us in such beautiful ways. You love us so much that You lead us as if we were blind and cannot see the way ahead. You will remove obstacles over which we will stumble and guide us around or through dangers that would hurt us. And even if I walk through the valley of the shadow of death, even if I am in times of acute distress, You are still with me, continuing to guard and guide me by Your love. (Isaiah 42:16.)

Lord, I thank You that regardless of the situation I am in, despite the difficulties I face, I know that You will lead me. I know that You will guide me. I know that You will bring me to Your "Oasis of Love" where I will know Your presence in a deep and intimate way.

Lord, I do not know many things. I do not know what uncertainties and difficulties I will have in the future. I do not know how I will get through my trials and troubles. I do not know what is going to happen tomorrow. But this one thing I do know, that You are the Lord, You are my Good Shepherd, You are my all-sufficiency. You are my guide forever and forever and forever and forever—for every single day of my life. Lord I lift up my voice to You and praise You. I lift up my heart in love and adoration to You. I lift up my life and put it into Your Hands. O Lord, how wonderful You are.

CHAPTER 5

PATHS OF BLESSING

He leads me in the paths of righteousness, for His Name's sake. (Psalm 23:3 NKJV.)

God loves us so much and takes great delight in us, and He just wants to lavish His blessings upon us. To do this He leads us in the paths of righteousness, and as we walk this way, He pours out His blessings upon us.

To "walk in the paths of righteousness" is not to live a life of obeying rules and regulations, but to live a life that is pleasing to God, doing His will. For example, when Jesus insisted on being baptised by John the Baptist, He said that He had to do it to "fulfil all righteousness". Then His Father blessed Him. The Holy Spirit came upon Him, and God spoke from heaven saying that Jesus was His Son whom He loved very much and He was very pleased with Him. For Jesus was obeying His Father's will. He was walking the paths of righteousness. (Matthew 3:13-16.)

Lord, I cannot walk with You unless I agree that Your way is right. I cannot follow You if I want to go my own way. Lord, I want to walk with You. I agree that Your paths are right and true. Help me to follow You. (Amos 3:3.)

Lord, You are righteous, holy and perfect. I am sinful, weak and imperfect. Lord, if I am to follow You, I need Your guidance. If I am to do those things that are pleasing to You then I need Your help. Otherwise, how can I, who am imperfect, walk the paths of perfection? How can I, who am sinful, walk the paths of holiness? How can I, who tends to do those things for my own pleasure, instead do those things that would please You? (1 Thessalonians 2:4; 1 John 3:22.)

Jesus, even You came into this world, not to please Yourself, but to please Your Father. You came not to do Your own will, but the will of Your Father. Help me to make this the goal in my life—to please You in every way. Lord, I put my hands into Yours. Lead me on in the right way; guide me on the correct path. (John 5:30; 6:38; 8:29; Matthew 26:39, 42; 2 Corinthians 5:9; Colossians 1:10.)

We must want to obey God from the heart. We must follow Him because we love Him. One evening, a boy remained standing up for a while in his home. Eventually he began to irritate his parents. Several times, they asked him to sit down but he refused. Then they told him to sit down, which he did, but he said, "I'm sitting down on the outside, but on the inside I'm still standing up!" We must please God, not because we have to, but because we want to, because we love Him.

Lord, help me to do Your will from my heart. Help me to do Your will with all of my soul. Then I know that You will lead me in the way that You want me to go—a way that is pleasing to You. Then I know that You will love me and You will come to me and show Yourself to me. And You will make Your home with me, and live with me. (Ephesians 6:6; John 14:21-23.)

Lord, search me so You will know my heart. Test me so You will know my thoughts. Examine me to see if there is any wicked way in me. Show me Lord, so I can turn to You from these things and ask You for help. And You will be so pleased with me You will lead me all the days of my life. So there will be no need for me to worry about what will happen in the future, because You will be leading me. I need not be anxious about any problems that will come because You will be helping me and guiding me. Lord, how wonderful You are. (Psalm 139:23-24.)

I thank You Jesus that when I sin, and confess it, You are faithful and just and will forgive me of my sin and cleanse me from all unrighteousness.

And You will do this so that I can continue to walk with You. And we will be together, walking hand in hand along life's way; just think about it—You and me, together, forever, Lord I praise You. (1 John 1:7, 9.)

Blessings of being led by God's Holy Spirit.

Lord, I thank You that because I am Your child, You give me the Holy Spirit. He will live with me. He will live in me. He will guide me into all truth, He will lead me, He will guide me, He will strengthen me, He will comfort me, He will counsel me. And He will witness with me that You—the Almighty God—You—the Holy One—You are my Father. (John 14:17, 26; 16:13; Romans 8:14.)

Lord, fill me with Your Holy Spirit. Help me to be led by Him. Then I will not have a life that is controlled by the power of sin, nor deeds dictated by the lusts of my flesh. As Your Spirit leads and guides me, then I know that I will live and walk in those ways that are pleasing to You. Then I will know Your approval and experience Your blessing flowing through me. (Romans 8:12-16.)

Lord, help me to be led by the Spirit. As He leads me, I will not be doing the acts of the sinful nature, but I will be filled with love, joy and peace—I will be walking the way that You want me to go. I will be walking step by step with You, in unison and in total agreement. We will be walking together, talking together, in fellowship with each other, enjoying each other's company. What a life that will be, I praise You Lord! (Galatians 5:25; 5:16-25.)

Blessings of walking on the paths of righteousness.

Lord, I thank You that when I hunger and thirst after righteousness, then I shall be blessed, enjoying Your favour upon my life. Lord as I earnestly desire to please You and to fulfil Your will for my life, then I will be filled with Your Holy Spirit, with Your peace and joy saturating me. As I yearn to walk along the paths of righteousness then I will be satisfied completely. (Matthew 5:6.)

Father, I thank You that when I seek first Your kingdom and Your righteousness, then I need not worry about anything in my life. For as do Your will, then I shall not want. As I please You then I need not worry about food, clothing or my health, or anything else, for You will add all these things to me. (Matthew 6:33, 25-34.)

Lord, as I walk uprightly before You, You will be my sun and shield. You will shine upon me to show me the way. You will protect me to keep me safe. As I walk along the paths of righteousness, You will show me Your love, and give me grace and glory. You will shower me with favour and blessing, filling me with peace and joy. As I walk with You, You will withhold no good thing from me. Lord how wonderful You are. As I trust You I am really blessed. (Psalm 84:11-12.)

For His Name's sake.

The condition of the sheep will display the care that the shepherd has for them. Those that are groomed, well fed and contented show that their shepherd cares for them and looks after their welfare. Sheep that look gaunt and unkempt show that their shepherd couldn't care less for them. Therefore, the condition of the sheep shows the character of the shepherd. So God, our All-Sufficient Shepherd, will lead us into green pastures. He will cause us to lie down beside the still waters. He will restore our soul and guide us in the paths of righteousness for His Name's sake. He blesses us in all our need, and as others see this, His Name will be glorified. He is our glory. His glory will be revealed in us. Others will see this and glorify God.

Lord, I trust in You. You are my rock, the sure foundation of my life. You are my fortress, my strength and my refuge. You are my deliverer, and You rescue me from my fears and worries. I have the confidence that You will help me, strengthen me, and guide me. I know that You will lead me. And I am certain that You will do this because You are my Shepherd and You care for me. And others will see Your love and compassion for me, and they will glorify You through what You have done for me. (Psalm 18:2; 31:3; 109:21.)

I thank You Lord that You brought Your children out of Egypt, Your presence went with them, You led them, You guided them, You provided for them, You gave them victories over their enemies. You had to do this because Your honour and reputation was at stake. Other nations were looking on, and had You not done these things for Your people then they would have mocked You. They would have thought You a weak and feeble God who could not look after His people. (Exodus 33:15-16; Psalm 79:10; Joel 2:17.)

I thank You Lord that You can save me from my depressions, anxieties, my worries and fears. You can strengthen me in all of my problems and help me in all of my troubles. You will do this because of Your wonderful love for me. You have to do this for Your Name's sake, so that others will see what You are doing for me and they will know how You are helping me. (Psalm 106:8; 109:21; 143:11.)

Jesus, I thank You that You have promised to answer my prayers so that You will bring glory to Your Father. You have promised to do anything I ask in Your Name so that all people will praise You. You have promised that if we stay close to You then You will give whatever we ask, so others will see how much You care for us and look after us and they will praise You. (John 14:13-14; 15:7-8.)

When I came out of church with some friends, a man was watching us. He came over and wanted to talk to the minister. He had noticed how happy all the people were, and he wanted to know why. The minister told him about Jesus.

I had a very memorable experience once. A young woman came to me when I was at work and wanted to know why I was so happy, for she had noticed me smiling a lot. I had the opportunity of telling her about Jesus. This was a remarkable moment, because two weeks later, she unexpectedly died.

Lord, I thank You that You forgive me of my sins, so that Your loving, merciful, gracious and forgiving character might be seen by others in me. And they will see how much You love me Jesus, for they will know You died on the cross for my sin. (1 John 2:12; Psalm 25:11.)

I thank You Lord that You keep all of Your promises for me through Your Son Jesus so that Your Name will be glorified in my life. Not one of Your promises fails. You do not allow one of them to fall to the ground.

Promises to forgive and pardon me of my sin.

Promises to help me in times of trouble.

Promises to comfort me in times of bereavement.

Promises to give me joy in times of sadness.

Promises to answer my prayers.

Promises to lead and guide me.

The promise of eternal life.

Promises to give me strength in times of weakness.

Promises to give me peace in times of uncertainty.

Promises that You will never leave nor forsake me . . .

O Lord, how wonderful are Your promises. How great You are in keeping them. Lord, continue to guide me on the paths of righteousness, for Your Name's sake. (2 Corinthians 1:20; 1 Samuel 3:19; 1 Kings 8:56.)

CHAPTER 6

GOD'S LOVING PRESENCE IN TROUBLED TIMES

Lord, I thank You that You are my Shepherd who will always love me, who will always help me, who will always be at my side, who will never leave nor forsake me, who will always care for me, so much the so that I shall not want.

Lord, I thank You that You will lead me into the "Oasis of Your Love" where I can lie down and rest with You, where I can eat of the green pastures and be fully satisfied and be content. There, I will find complete refreshment and You will restore my soul.

Lord, I thank You that You will always lead me on the paths of righteousness, paths of rich blessing, where I will enjoy Your favour on my life, and I will experience the fullness of Your joy and peace flowing through me.

Lord, I thank You that wherever You lead me, it will be for "Your Name's sake". I thank You that whatever situation You lead me through it will be to glorify Your Name. It will be so that others will see Your wonderful love and amazing blessing flowing through me, that they shall glorify You. You will so fill me with Your peace and joy that others will see how much that You really care for me.

Lord, I thank You that You are my Good Shepherd who knows the way I should go, and You will always lead me along the right path. Lord, I thank You that You know the paths that are best for me, and You will guide me along them. I thank You Lord that You will always be with me to help me go the way that You have chosen for me.

Lord, some of the paths You lead me through are a bit hard to walk on. But I thank You that You will always uphold me with Your hand and hold me close to Your heart. So even though I do not understand why You have asked me to go on some difficult ways, I know that I can always trust You. (Psalm 37:24; Isaiah 40:11.)

Yea, even though I walk through the valley of the shadow of death, I will fear no evil, for You are with me. (Psalm 23:4 NKJV.)

The valley of the shadow of death is an expression for the blackest darkness. It gives the idea of a place where there is no light shining, where darkness seems to rule and apparently has dominion. It is a place where there is no order, and where it seems that the light is like darkness. (Job 10:21-22.) An object coming between the light and the sun casts a long, gloomy and dark shadow. It speaks not only of death itself, but also of a path of gloom or sadness, scenes of trouble and trials, places of solitude and sorrow. It describes a place of discouragement, defeat, depression and despondency, where apparently no light is shining and there seems to be no hope for the future. Death stands between life and us. It casts its shadow over us so that we cannot see the light, nor expect to receive life.

Lord, sometimes You ask me to walk through the valley of the shadow of death. But I thank You Lord that in this valley You are with me and You will never leave nor forsake me. I thank You Lord that as I seek You I will find Your comfort. I thank You Lord that I need fear no evil.

Lord, I thank You that you will walk with me through the valley of the shadow of death. I thank You Lord that I am not walking in the valley but "through" it. You will bring me through it, and out of it, into the glorious sunshine of life on the other side. I thank You Lord that the place that You will bring me into is a bountiful place where there is much fruit to eat and good things to experience. (Jeremiah 2:6-7.)

Lord, there are times when I go through the darkest and gloomiest of situations, when there seems to be no light. Yet, Lord, I thank You that this is still the right path for me. I thank You Lord that in these situations, as I trust You, I will know Your presence; I will know Your help; I will know Your comfort.

Lord, there are those difficult times when I do not know what is happening. Lord, there are those hard times when I get hurt and upset. Lord, there are those times when I get down and don't know what to do. But I do thank You Lord, that You are at my side, that You always love me, and even though I do not understand what is happening, I can always trust You. I can always keep my eyes fixed upon You—for from You will come my help. (2 Chronicles 20:12; Psalm 121:1-2.)

Lord, there are some times when I am almost overwhelmed by despair and despondency. There are times when I am weak and I feel that I am at the end of my tether. But I thank You Lord that You will help me, You will never let me go, You will lift me up and You will strengthen me. (John 10:28-29; Psalm 30:1; 145:14; Isaiah 40:29-31.)

I thank You Lord that in all times and situations, in trouble and hardships, in difficulty or dangers, nothing can separate me from Your love. I thank You Lord that although I will have troubles, You will not allow anything to come upon me to overwhelm me. But in every situation, You will give me strength to get through the problem with victory. You will make me more than a conqueror. (1 Corinthians 10:13; Romans 8:35-39.)

Lord I thank You for the wonderful position I am in, even if I am in the valley of the shadow of death, for there will never be a moment when You are not at my side. There will never be a second when You will not be my guide. You are always ahead of me leading the way. Lord, Your goodness and mercy will always be following me. There will never be a day when You are not behind me. Lord, You are always with me; You are continually at my side. What a wonderful God You are. Always leading me—always following me—always with me at my side! (Psalm 23:3-6.)

Unhealthy fear is a destructive force. It produces physical changes, such as sweating, increased heart rate and blood pressure. It can produce mental instability, which can lead to mental illness. It can produce stress, which could lead to death.

During the Gulf war of 1991, Iraq attacked Israel with missiles. After the war, scientists examined those who died. They found that most of deaths that occurred in the first day of attacks were not as a result from any direct physical attacks of the missiles, but from heart failure brought on through fear and stress caused by worrying about the possibility of being hit. [d]

An earthquake hit Los Angeles in January 1994. A cardiologist at one of the hospitals, Robert Kloner, noted that over 100 people literally died of fright rather than any immediate effect of the earthquake. [e]

Lord, there are times when it seems that evil is in control and there seems to be no hope and no future. But, I thank You Lord that You are with me. The path through the valley of the shadow of death is still a path of safety; it is a path where I will find Your strength and comfort. It is a path where I will fear no evil, but I will know Your help and victory. I thank You Lord that You have plans and thoughts for me, plans to give me hope, thoughts to give me a future. (Jeremiah 29:11.)

I thank You Lord that You are my light and my salvation. You will shine upon me when I am in dark, gloomy and difficult situations. Therefore, when I am in the valley of the shadow of death, I will see a great light. I will not fear for You will guide my feet in the path of peace. (Luke 1:79; Matthew 4:16; Psalm 27:1.)

Lord, I thank You that in those dark and difficult times I will fear no evil, for You are at my side. I thank You Lord that although at times the way is hard and the experience distressing, I have nothing to fear, for You are with me. You are my constant companion and faithful friend. You are always my skilful guide and my protective guardian. You will never leave me. You will never forsake me. Nothing can separate me from Your love. No one can pluck me from Your hand—no one can take me from my Father's hand. (John 10:28-29.)

I thank You Lord that You are with me, therefore I will not be afraid. I thank You Father that You are my refuge and strength, You are an ever-present help in times of trouble, therefore I will not fear. I thank You Lord that as I "walk" through the valley of the shadow of death, I need not flee away because of fear. I need not panic because of worry or anxiety. I need not wring my hands in horror or dread. Instead, I am walking calmly and fearlessly with You, my Good Shepherd, at my side. (Psalm 46:1-2; 118:6.)

Lord, I thank You for as You lead me on the paths of righteousness, then You are leading me on the paths of blessing, where You will fill me with Your love. And if this path of righteousness takes me through the valley of the shadow of death, I will not fear because Your love that fills me will cast out all fear. (1 John 4:18.)

Lord, I am confident that You will continue to guide me through the valley of the shadow of death. I am absolutely certain that You will walk with me at my side. I am totally confident that You will help me because of "Your Name's sake". Other people will see me going through difficulties, and as they will see You helping me through them, they will glorify Your Name.

I thank You Lord that You are with me, so I need not fear. I thank You Lord that You are my God, so I need not be dismayed. You will strengthen me, You will help me; You will uphold me with Your hand. You call me by my name. I am Yours; I belong to You. When I pass through the waters, You will be with me. When I pass through the rivers, they will not sweep over me. When I walk through the fire, I will not be burned; the flames will not set me ablaze, for I am precious to You. I am honoured in Your sight. You love me. I need not fear. (Isaiah 41:10; 43:1-4.)

Chapter 7

The Lord, My Wonderful Comforter

Yea, though I walk through the valley of the shadow of death, I will fear no evil; For You are with me; Your rod and Your staff, they comfort me (Psalm 23:4 NKJV).

Lord, I thank You that as I walk on the path You have chosen for me, the path of righteousness, You will lavish Your blessing upon me in a wonderful way. You will pour out upon me Your love. You will fill me to overflowing with Your joy. Your peace will flood into my mind. Lord, how wonderful You are.

I thank You Lord that You will always lead me into the "Oasis of Love". There I shall find rest and refreshment. There I will be safe and secure. There I shall be enjoying Your presence, basking in the sunshine of Your love. There You will be singing over me with songs of joy, enjoying my company.

Lord, I thank You that even if this path leads me through the valley of the shadow of death, You will always be with me having fellowship with me. You will always be at my side to guard and protect me. You will always be ahead of me, leading and guiding me.

In the valley of the shadow of death—Your rod and Your staff, they comfort me.

A person who shows comfort to someone means that he has seen the problems others have, and feels sorry for them. He shows compassion by coming to them, to be with them, to help them, to strengthen them and to encourage them. He replaces the negative feelings of sorrow and sadness with joy and hope. In calling Isaiah to "Comfort my people", God wants the people to receive calmness in the middle of affliction, joy in the middle of sorrow, strength in the middle of weakness, and also to receive the brightest of hopes for the future. (Isaiah 40:1-2.)

Father, I thank You that You are the God of all comfort. You are the source of all comfort, the fountain from which all happiness, strength and encouragement flows. Lord, there is no other source of real comfort. There is no other place I can go; no other person I can turn to, where I can be consoled, receive comfort, relief, help and blessing. (2 Corinthians 1:3; 7:6.)

Lord, I thank You that from You I will receive comfort in all my troubles, I will obtain strength in all my afflictions, I will be consoled in all my tribulations. Lord, I am truly blessed because there is no difficulty where You will not comfort me, no trial where You cannot strengthen me. For in all my problems, You will comfort me, You will hold me close to Your heart, You will strengthen me, You will carry me through. Lord I love You. (2 Corinthians 1:4.)

Lord, I thank You that when You give comfort, You impart positive benefits and powerful blessings. You come alongside those who are broken hearted and heal them. You come to those who are imprisoned by depression and despondency and free them. You put Your arms around those who mourn and pour Your joy into them. (Isaiah 61:1-3.)

Lord, I thank You that You will comfort me when I am downcast, and give me joy and encouragement. When I am in despair You will come to me, lift me up, carry me and give me peace. When anxiety, worries and fears press down upon me, You will help me, You will lift my burdens and give me rest. (Matthew 11:29-30; 2 Corinthians 7:6.)

Lord, when You comfort me I will be strong and stable and I will praise You for Your love and comfort, and I will thank You for Your goodness and mercy. And You will be glorified in my life, because You did it for "Your Name's sake". (Isaiah 61:3.)

And Lord, the comfort that You give me is so great and wonderful that I will be able to comfort others. I will not just be able to tell them about Your wonderful comfort, but with Your love flowing through me, You will enable me to impart Your love into their lives so they may experience Your love and receive Your comfort. (2 Corinthians 1:4-6.)

The rod and staff are the shepherd's tools. They speak of God's love and tender care towards us. They are symbols of His support, His comfort, care and protection.

The staff was a straight stick or pole. The shepherd used the staff to ward off animals that imposed a danger to the sheep. He could throw it and kill the predators. The shepherd would also go before the sheep to lead them into green pasture. Before they settled down in the pasture, he would walk through it using the staff to flush out snakes from the grass and kill them, and then they could eat and rest in safety having no fear of any danger.

Lord, I thank You that I am a sheep in Your flock and I belong to You. I am very precious to You. You treasure me and delight to be with me. You continually look over me to protect me and guard me. You cover me with Your love and protect me by Your power, and underneath me are Your everlasting arms. Because You are always with me, You are my shield and my shelter, my refuge and my fortress. You are my refuge and underneath me are Your everlasting arms. You will drive away my enemy and defeat him. (Psalm 91:4; Deuteronomy 33:27.)

Lord, because You love me and value me very highly, You surround me with Your presence both now and forevermore. You set around me Your angels to watch over me. They will protect and deliver me. They will watch over me and guard me. They will defend and keep me. They will lift me up in their hands. (Psalm 34:7; 91:11-12; 125:2; 2 Kings 6:16-17; Matthew 18:10.)

As I look to You Lord, I know that You care for me; I know that You are always with me. I know that You will defend me and protect me, guide me and guard me. In this alone, I find comfort. But I know that whatever happens in the future, You will be with me, You will look after me, in every situation and at every moment, and in this I can face the future knowing that You will be with me to help and comfort me.

The rod was the shepherd's crook, curved at one end. If a sheep had fallen into a gulley or ravine, then he would reach the sheep with his rod. Then with the curved part, he would encircle part of the sheep's body and lift it to safety. At the end of the day, he would use it to count the sheep. As he counted them, he caused them to pass, one by one, under the rod and examined them carefully to see if they were well. (Leviticus 27:32; Ezekiel 20:37.)

Lord, I love You, and I trust in Your unfailing love and mercy. I thank You that You watch over me, every moment of the day, to deliver and keep me, in good times and bad. Lord, I trust You and rely upon You, for You are my shield and defender, You are my present help, especially in times of trouble. (Psalm 33:18-22; 46:1.)

Lord, I thank You that You are always at my side. When I stumble, You are there to hold and strengthen me so I do not fall. When I do fall, I shall not be utterly cast down, for You grab me by the hand, You pick me up and hold me close. (Psalm 37:24; 145:14.)

Lord, You care for me so much that Your eyes are always upon me, Your ears are always open to all my prayers. You know all about me. Even the small things do not escape your attention—You will notice even the smallest teardrop that trickles from my eye. You pay great attention to me so that you will hear not just my prayers but also every sigh that comes from my heart. (Matthew 10:30; 1 Peter 3:12.)

Lord, You know when I am not well, You know when I am burdened, You know when I am anxious. You see all things—You know all things. I thank You Lord that You do not stand idly by, but You are at my side to help me, to heal me, to comfort me, to lift me, to strengthen me. O Lord, how wonderful You are.

Lord, when I walk through the valley of the shadow of death, You are with me, You are continually at my side, You will never leave nor forsake me and I will fear no evil.

Lord, as I journey through this life, Your rod and Your staff, they will comfort me. You will keep me safe from danger, You will protect and guard me, and underneath me are Your everlasting arms. You will strengthen me, You will uphold me, You will bless me, You will always hold me close to Your heart.

Lord, I will break forth into joy; I will burst into songs of praise. For You Lord are my comforter. In every situation, in every trial, in every difficulty, You Lord are with me to comfort me, to bless me, to encourage and strengthen me. I will continually lift my eyes and heart to You, Lord, my comforter and deliverer. (Isaiah 52:9.)

CHAPTER 8

A LOVE FEAST

You prepare a table before me in the presence of my enemies. (Psalm 23:5 NKJV.)

Lord, I thank You that every day You will guide me on the paths of righteousness, where I shall walk with You. On this path, we will have fellowship and enjoy being together. For You love me with an everlasting love, and You take great delight in being with me. Lord, my heart and life are forever Yours.

Lord, I thank You that You will always lead me to Your "Oasis of Love", where I will be fully satisfied and completely content. There, I will lie down and rest in Your presence, rejoicing in Your love. There, You will restore my soul.

Lord, even if the path You lead me on will take me into the valley of the shadow of death, You will still be with me, at my side. You will never leave me nor forsake me. Therefore, I will not be afraid. Nothing can separate me from Your love; no one can pluck me out of Your hand.

Lord, even in these difficult times when on this dark path, You will always comfort, protect and guard me. You will always care for me, look over me and look after me. You will continue to carry me, lovingly holding me close to Your heart.

Lord, I know that You will lead me through this dark valley, and You will bring me out of it into Your "Oasis of Love", where You have prepared a table before me.

You, my Shepherd, have prepared a table before me.

The Hebrew word used for "table" describes the sort of table used for a king. [a] *Therefore the feast will be sumptuous, like a magnificent banquet. Phrases like super abundance, amazing excess, incredibly large quantity and unsurpassable quality would have to be used to describe it. This is how the Lord, our Shepherd, wants to provide for His children, His flock. His provisions for us far exceed our expectations.*

Lord, I thank You that this table is prepared for "me". While You love all of Your children, You are interested in every individual person and that includes me. You are concerned about me. You love me. You know my name. You even know the number of hairs on my head, and because You know the things that are of small importance, You know everything about me. You know all my needs and all my cares. (John 10:3, 14, 27; Luke 12:6-7.)

Lord, I thank You that because You have prepared this table for "me", it is furnished to meet my own individual needs. You have the key to unlock the solution to my every problem. You know how to help me in every situation. You know how to meet my every need. The contents of the table You have furnished for me are "tailor made". You love me so much that You have provided just what I need.

Lord, I thank You that the table is already prepared for me, and it is ready for me before I need it! Lord, You know the things that I have need of, even before I ask You, and sometimes You answer before I ask! Before I say anything, You know all of what I am going to say. You know my thoughts even before they come into my mind. Lord, You are absolutely amazing, and Your love for me is wonderful. (Psalm 139:4; Isaiah 65:24; Matthew 6:8.)

I praise You Lord, for as I come to You telling You about a problem I have, or about a need I've got, You already know about it, and You have the answer already at hand. Lord, You are just waiting for me to come to You and trust You.

I thank You Lord that You think of me so much that you prepare for me a table that is fit for a king. You have prepared for me a sumptuous banquet that far exceeds all that I need. It is a love feast. You love me so much that Your grace super-abounds to me. You pour out Your grace upon me in an exceedingly abundant way. For Your grace is sufficient for my every need. (2 Corinthians 12:9; Romans 5:20; 1 Timothy 1:14.)

I thank You Lord that You pour Your love into my heart, You fill me to full and overflowing with a glorious and triumphant joy that I cannot put my feelings into words. You super fill me with such an enormous and marvellous peace that far exceeds all my understanding. You will generously and abundantly meet all of my needs according to Your infinite glorious riches in Christ Jesus. (Romans 5:5; 15:13; 1 Peter 1:8; Philippians 4:7, 19.)

I thank You Lord that the table is prepared "before" me. It is spread in my presence, in front of me. I do not have to strive to get to it for it is in my reach. I do not have to do anything to achieve it for it is already there for me. You have prepared the feast because You love me. I come to You Lord, and You will quench my thirst. I seek after You Lord, and You will satisfy my hunger. I ask of You Lord and You will meet all of my need. (John 7:37-38; Matthew 5:6; 6:33; 7:7-11.)

Lord, I thank You that when I am in difficult situations, when I have troubles, when I am in despair, You are able to spread for me a table in my "desert" situation. In this desert, You can cause streams of water to flow abundantly to quench my thirst. You can supply meat to satisfy my hunger. For You will bring me to Your "Oasis of Love", where I will rest and be satisfied, and where You will meet my every need. (Psalm 78:19-25.)

Lord, I praise You for when I walk through the valley of the shadow of death, You are there with me so I will not fear, You will comfort me so I will be strengthened and encouraged. You will bring me through the valley to the table You have prepared, to Your "Oasis of Love".

The table is prepared in the presence of my enemies.

Before the shepherd brings his flock into the pasture, he looks out for any poisonous plants, which could be fatal for the grazing animals, and removes them. He puts them on top of stones to dry out so that they could be burned the next day. He looks out for any snakes that would be hiding in holes or lying camouflaged in the grass. He looks out for other predators, which would attack the sheep and kill them. Then he leads the sheep into the new pasture that he has prepared. In the presence of their enemies, the dead weeds and slain predators, they eat to their full, in safety and peace. The sheep would not be worried about any surprise attacks from the snakes, nor the brutal attacks from lions or bears. They know that their shepherd was more than capable of dealing with any enemy.

Lord Jesus, I thank You that through Your death at the cross and Your resurrection, You have the victory over all my enemies. You have publically disarmed all the powers that were against me, powers of worry, depression, anxiety, fear, and all that would try to defeat me and destroy my life. You have defeated Satan, destroyed his work, and conquered death. (Colossians 2:15; Hebrews 2:14; 1 John 3:8.)

Lord, I do rejoice in Your victory, for I know that absolutely nothing can separate me from Your love, be it death or anything in this life, be it angels or demons, be it any power or person. Lord, I am convinced beyond any doubt that nothing in all of this creation, be it in the present or in the future, can separate me from You. (Romans 8:38-39.)

I praise You for Your victory Lord, because I know that nothing can snatch me from Your hand, because You have all power over all my enemies. And I praise You that no one can take me from my Father's hand because He is greater and mightier than all. (John 10:28-29.)

Therefore Lord, when I walk through the valley of the shadow of death, and my enemies are round about me, I thank You that You, the Victorious One, are with me. I thank You that You, the All-Conquering One, are leading me, and I need not fear. For You, the Triumphant One, care for me and give me comfort.

Lord, I rejoice that my enemies cannot stop You from preparing the table for me, and they cannot stop me from coming to You and taking my provision from the table. I can rest and enjoy the feast. I can take time in Your presence, receiving blessing upon blessing, grace upon grace, and strength upon strength.

I thank You Lord that when I am harassed by the enemy, under stress from my circumstances, pressured by temptations, persecuted by others, I can come to You, my All-Sufficient Shepherd, and eat from the table that You have already prepared for me.

Lord, I thank You for Your wonderful presence with me in the valley of the shadow of death. You are there with me because You love me. I love You Lord.

Lord, I thank You for the magnificent banquet You have prepared before me on the table in the presence of my enemies. You have provided this for me because You care for me. I adore You Lord.

Lord, I thank You that You will always lead me into the "Oasis of Love" in the middle of the desert. You do this because I am the apple of Your eye, precious in Your sight and dearly loved. I worship You Lord.

CHAPTER 9

AN ANOINTING

You anoint my head with oil; my cup runs over. (Psalm 23:5 NKJV.)

When the sheep come into the sheepfold at night, the shepherd will make them come in by a certain gate. Here, the shepherd will have to hand a large bowl of olive oil and a large jar of water. As the sheep enter, one by one, the shepherd will make them go under his rod as he counts them. He also examines each one to see if there are any cuts or other injuries. If so, he takes the sheep to one side where he cleanses the wound and anoints the injury with the oil. For the shepherd does not want today's wound to become tomorrow's infection. (Leviticus 27:32; Jeremiah 33:13.)

Lord, I thank You for Your loving concern for me. You will always affectionately care for me. Your eyes are always upon me. Your ears are always open to my prayers. You will continually gaze lovingly over me. Wherever I go, whatever I do, You will watch over me, You will look after me, You will protect me, now and for the rest of my life. (1 Peter 3:12; Psalm 121:7-8.)

Lord, I do love You. You take an intimate interest in me. You take time to be with me. You know all about my life. Indeed Lord, You know me better than I know myself—for You always know the number of hairs on my head! Lord, I know that You are always with me, You know everything about me—no matter how big or how small—because You care for me. (Luke 12:7.)

I thank You Lord that there is never a moment when You are not with me. There is never a moment that You do not care for me. You do not miss hearing my prayers—not even the quietest sigh or groan. You do not miss seeing any tear that trickles down my cheeks. And You know, You love, You care.

I thank You Lord that You are a God of compassion, love and comfort and You comfort and strengthen me in all of my troubles. When I am broken hearted, You heal me. When I am depressed, You will deliver and free me. When I mourn, You will comfort me. When I am weak, You will strengthen me. When I am cast down, You will lift me up. You are always with me so that I can cast my life, with all of its anxieties, worries and cares upon You. (2 Corinthians 1:3-4; Isaiah 61:1-2; Luke 4:18; 1 Peter 5:7.)

When distinguished guests came to a meal their host would have their heads anointed with oil. This is an expression of honour. It would also refresh the guests and prepare them to enjoy the meal. When Jesus was at a meal Mary came to Him and poured very costly ointment on His head and feet. She did this because, in her eyes, Jesus was very special, and she expressed her feelings of love and adoration to Him. Jesus said that this was a beautiful act. (Matthew 26:6-7; Mark 14:8; John 12:3.)

Lord, I thank You that Your love for me is beautiful and wonderful. It is a love that knows no limit. It is a love that knows no end. It is a love that does not depend on me. I cannot earn it nor deserve it. Your love for me will never cease nor diminish. It is an eternal and everlasting love. I thank You that You will always remain faithful to me and I can continually trust and depend upon You. (Jeremiah 31:3; John 17:23.)

I thank You Lord that I am the apple of Your eye—extremely precious to You. Therefore, You will continually watch over me, You will always look after me and care for me because You think so highly of me. (Deuteronomy 32:10.)

I thank You God that in Your sight, I am so beautiful—like a glorious sparkling jewel. Indeed, You see me as amazingly beautiful, like a magnificent royal crown. You hold me in Your hand, and You see me as so marvellous that You hold me up for all to see. (Isaiah 62:2-3; Zechariah 9:16.)

I thank You Lord that Your love for me is like a bridegroom's love for the bride. Therefore, You take great delight over me and You rejoice over me. You love me so much that You enjoy being with me, and You sing over me with joy. (Isaiah 62:4-5; Zephaniah 3:17.)

Lord, I thank You that You are my All-Sufficient Shepherd. I can rest content with You knowing that even in the presence of my enemies You have prepared a table before me. For I am with You in the "Oasis of Love". Here I am at the centre of Your intimate love and devoted affection.

David declared that God has anointed his head with oil. When the priests were anointed with oil, it was poured upon their head, it then ran down their beards and then over the rest of them. (Psalm 133:2.) Therefore, the anointing will affect and touch every part of their lives.

I thank You Lord that when You anoint me with oil, it will be like the priests in the Old Testament days, when it was poured upon their head, ran down their beards and then all over. Therefore, Your anointing will affect all of me and touch every single part of my life. (Psalm 133:2.)

I thank You Lord that You anoint me with the Holy Spirit. I thank You Lord that You give the Holy Spirit without limit, and You will pour Him upon me generously. I thank You Lord that You will completely and continually fill me with the Holy Spirit. (John 3:34; 20:21-22; Acts 2:17, 33; Ephesians 5:18; Titus 3:5-6.)

Lord, I thank You that Your Holy Spirit will give my mortal body life, abundant life, victorious life. You will give me strength in place of weakness, victory in place of defeat, health in place of sickness, love in place of fear. (Romans 5:5; 8:11, 15; Ephesians 3:16.)

This anointing is symbolic of prosperity, joy and the fact that God's favour rests upon His people. The word in Psalm 23:5 for "anoint" comes from a Hebrew word that means "to make fat, to satisfy, to make prosperous." The word is used for one's bones made fat (in good health) after receiving good news. (Proverbs 15:30). *(a)* *The generous, diligent and those who trust in the Lord are described as "fat" or "prosperous." (b) The NIV also translates it as "prosper" or "fully satisfied." (Proverbs 11:25; 13:4; 28:25.) The blessing or anointing of God upon is so abundant that we are completely satisfied and makes us prosperous.*

I thank You Lord that Your anointing upon me is without measure. Your blessing upon me is so abundant that it makes me more than satisfied. Lord, Your anointing and blessing upon my life causes me to prosper. It makes me thrive and flourish. It is as if I were "made fat" with it. (Psalm 23:5.)

I thank You Lord that You have prepared for me a table—it will satisfy all my needs. You have so abundantly anointed me that blessing upon blessing pours down upon me. You have led me into Your "Oasis of Love". I can relish and feast on the abundance that You supply me and can drink from the stream of Your pleasures and delights. (Psalm 36:8.)

Let us look at just two areas of our lives that God's rich blessing is upon—prosperity and joy. The first one considered is prosperity.

He made him ride on the high places of the earth, that he might eat the increase of the fields; and he made him to suck honey out of the rock, and oil out of the flinty rock (Deuteronomy 32:13 KJV).

God promised Israel that He would nourish him with honey from the rock, and with oil from the flinty rock. (Deuteronomy 32:13.) Honey out of the rock and oil out of the flinty rock speaks of the most valuable productions out of the most unproductive places. God's blessing upon the land is so colossal that it seemed that the very rocks and stones were productive. This illustration comes from these two facts. The wild bees that lived in the Promise Land made their hives in the clefts of the rock. God would cause these bees to abound in number so much that it was as if "honey came from the rock". God would also cause the olive trees that grew in the rocky soil to flourish that it was as if "oil came from the flinty rock".

I thank You Lord that Your blessing upon me is immense. It is like being nourished by honey that comes out of a rock and oil from the flinty rock.

Your blessing upon me will be so colossal that in all the areas of my life I struggle in, I will be so blessed and will receive immense satisfaction.

Lord, I praise You for Your light will shine in my darkness. Your comfort will bless me in my difficult times. Your joy will fill me during my sorrowful moments. You will give me strength in times of weakness, peace in times of turmoil, hope in times of uncertainty, gladness in times of hardship and Your presence will be with me in times of suffering.

Lord, even if I go through the valley of the shadow of death, You will always lead me through it and bring me to a table on which you have prepared for me a sumptuous feast. Whenever I go through a desert experience, you will always bring me into Your "Oasis of Love". There, with You, I will lie down, extremely content and completely satisfied. Lord, how wonderful You are.

Another area where God's blessing is upon us is joy. The anointing that was upon Jesus was the "oil of exultant joy and gladness". This indicates that the anointing poured upon Him was of a superabundant joy. (Psalm 45:7; Hebrews 1:9.)

Lord Jesus, I thank You as I remain in Your presence, Your superabundant joy shall be in me, my gladness will know no measure and my joy shall be full, complete and overflowing. (John 15:11.)

Lord, I thank You that You will fill me with this joy in times of difficulty and trials. It is a joy that is inexpressible, unspeakable and glorious. It will so fill me that I will be unable to explain how absolutely wonderful I feel. (1 Peter 1:6-8.)

I thank You Lord that when I'm with You, everlasting joy will crown my head. I will experience gladness and have a joy that will overtake me. Sorrow and sighing will flee away. You will fill my heart with Your joy, which is my strength. (Isaiah 35:10; Nehemiah 8:10; Acts 14:17.)

In Psalm 16:11 the Hebrew word for "fullness" in "fullness of joy" means fullness, abundance, satisfaction. It refers to a state of saturation, over fullness, being stuffed—in a good sense! [a]

I thank You Lord that in Your presence is fullness of joy. So as I spend time with You I will be "overfilled or completely stuffed" with Your joy. Your joy in me will be such that there will be no room for anything else, be it sadness or sorrow, grief or gloom or any other negative feeling. In fact, Lord, Your joy will pour out from me and will affect others! (Psalm 16:11.)

I thank You Lord that You will anoint me with the oil of joy, and this joy will replace all mourning and sadness. You will clothe me with the garments of praise instead of heaviness. You will deliver me from all despondency and grief. (Isaiah 61:1-3.)

A friend of mine worked in the police force in the Midlands, and there was a time when he was going through very difficult and testing circumstances. One day, he was riding to work on his motorbike when suddenly and unexpectedly the anointing of God came upon him. God filled him with such a phenomenal joy that it became impossible to ride on his bike safely. He pulled over to one side and stopped, and remained there for a while rejoicing in the presence of God.

David then declared that God has anointed his head with oil and that He has poured out so many blessings upon him that his cup overflowed. In Bible times, the overflowing cup was a powerful symbol. If the cup sat empty, the host was hinting that it was time to go. If the cup was kept full, the guest was welcome. If he really enjoyed your company, however, he kept filling it until it ran over the edge and down on to the table.

I thank You Lord that my cup is not just filled to the brim, but it overflows. The blessings You pour out upon me are abundant, extravagant and excessive. Your blessings are not just a saturation but also a deluge!

I thank you Lord that I am so precious to You that You enjoy being with me. You love me so much that You want me to remain in Your presence. Therefore, You continually keep my cup full and overflowing. Your grace will continue to overflow to me and in me. Your joy will continue to overflow. Your love will continue to super abound.

Lord, I thank You that there will never be a moment when the cup will cease to be full and overflowing, for You never will reject me, You will never turn me away, You will never make me feel unwelcome or unwanted. Lord, how great is Your love to me.

I thank You Jesus that You came so that I may have and enjoy life and have it in such an unlimited abundance that it overflows. (John 10:10.)

I thank You Jesus that You do not give the Holy Spirit sparingly, or by measure in dribs and drabs. You give the Holy Spirit in a boundless way, without any limit. You will fill me so much with Your Holy Spirit that, like a torrent, He will flow out continuously from my inner most being. (John 3:34; 7:37-39.)

I thank You Jesus that You give me Your superabundant joy. I thank You Lord that my joy will be of full measure, complete and overflowing. Even in times of trial, You will fill me with a joy that is inexpressible, unspeakable and full of glory. (John 15:11; 1 Peter 1:6-8.)

I thank You Jesus that You are my All-Sufficient Shepherd. You will lead me into Your "Oasis of Love". You will bring me to a sumptuous feast that You have already provided for me—a magnificent banquet that will more than meet my need. You will anoint my head with oil; You will cause my cup to brim over and overflow with Your superabundant blessings. Lord, how wonderful You are.

Chapter 10

Heavenly Sheepdogs

Surely goodness and mercy shall follow me all the days of my life.
(Psalm 23:6 NKJV.)

God has two "sheepdogs", one called Goodness and the other called Mercy. They follow us all the days of our life, making sure that we do not stray from, but that we stay on, the correct path. They will always be with us, looking after us, guiding and warning us. They will always be there, with us, making sure that we will dwell in the House of the Lord forever—where we will be with the Lord.

The word "surely" has an emphatic sense that conveys the meaning of certainty, assurance and confidence.

I thank You Lord that I can be absolutely certain and have no doubt at all that Your goodness and mercy shall follow me all the days of my life. Regardless of the circumstances I am in, I know that Your goodness and mercy will follow me during these times, regardless of how I feel.

I thank You Lord that even if I am walking through the valley of the shadow of death, I have the absolute assurance that Your goodness and unfailing love are following me. They will continue to lead me and take me to the table that You have prepared for me.

I praise You Lord, that when it seems that I am having a desert experience, and I'm struggling in my life, because You are my Good Shepherd, Your goodness and mercy are following me. They will continue to guide me and bring me into the "Oasis of Love". There I shall lie down in the green pastures; there will I be beside the still waters. There shall I be with You.

I thank You Lord that if the enemy is around me, I know without any doubt—I have the concrete certainty—that Your goodness and mercy are following me, keeping me, guarding and guiding me. And I will come to the table, for in the presence of my enemies You have prepared for me a sumptuous feast; You will anoint my head with oil; You will cause my cup to overflow.

I thank You Lord that because You are my All-Sufficient Shepherd, Provider and Friend there is no argument, no uncertainty and no doubt that Your goodness and mercy shall follow me for the rest of my life.

The word "surely" also has a restrictive sense, meaning that goodness and mercy only, and nothing else, shall follow me. [a]

I thank You Lord that if I am walking through the valley of the shadow of death and look behind me to see what is following me, I will not see depression and despair but only goodness and mercy.

I thank You Lord that if my foes are pursuing me, when I look over my shoulder I will not see defeat and despondency, but I will see only Your goodness and mercy following me.

I thank You Jesus that because You are my Good Shepherd, who has laid Your life down for me, it is impossible to consider that anything else will follow me except for Your goodness and mercy.

I thank You God that Your goodness and mercy are so great and vast that they will envelop any troubles and trials I have. Your goodness and mercy are so mighty and powerful that they will overcome the enemy and all that he throws at me.

I thank You Jesus that as I look behind me, I shall only see Your eternal goodness and mercy, for all other things are nothing in their sight. Your mercy and goodness are so beautiful and wonderful that they will bring me fullness of peace and overflowing joy in the midst of difficulties. (2 Corinthians 4:18.)

The meaning of the word "follow" is to run after, to chase, hunt or pursue. The basic meaning is "to pursue after" an enemy with the aim of overtaking and defeating him. It is like the leopard that follows his prey having the sole intent of catching the prey, overcoming and destroying it.

I thank You Lord that Your goodness and mercy will follow me with the intention of catching me and overwhelming me. They will never stop following me. They will never give up pursuing me until they catch me up and bless me in wonderful ways.

I thank You Lord that You have such a passion to bless me, that You eagerly follow me, even when I veer off the right path, and You will not stop coming after me until You catch me and bring me back to the right path, so that You can hold me close to Your heart.

I thank You Lord that when I listen to You and obey You, when I follow You, then blessing after blessing after blessing will come upon me, overtake me and overwhelm me. (Deuteronomy 28:2.)

Lord, I thank You that these blessings will touch every part of my life. Your promises will come to pass. You will bless me in all circumstances and in all situations. You will bless me in good and hard times. Your blessing on me shall be so great that it will touch the lives of those around me. (Deuteronomy 28:1-14.)

The word "good" can describe something that is pleasant or delightful.
An event or circumstance is said to be "good" when it is favourable or brings benefit.
An activity is said to be "good" when it brings pleasure or delight to someone.
"Good" describes a person's well-being of joyfulness or happiness.

I thank You God that Your very nature and character is good. Everything about You is good. Everything You say is good; everything You do is good;

everything You give is good; everything You created was not just good but "very good". (1 Kings 8:56; Acts 10:38; James 1:17; Matthew 7:11; Genesis 1:31.)

I thank You Jesus that You are my Good Shepherd. I thank You Lord that because You are good You cannot be anything else but good; You cannot do anything else but good; You cannot say anything else but good, otherwise You would be denying Your character and You would cease to be God. (John 10:11.)

So God, You pursue me because You are good. You pursue me because You love me and want to be with me. You follow me because You want to bring pleasure and delight to my life, and bestow on me good things and lead me in good paths.

Because You are good, all Your promises are good. They encourage me. They help me in my life. You have promised always to be with me. You have promised to guide me. You have promised to answer my prayers. You have promised to strengthen, help and comfort me. So many promises, and not one word of Your good promises have failed. (1 Kings 8:56.)

Because You are good, You answer Your children's prayers and give good gifts to those that ask You. You will give things that will benefit and help me in every area of my life. Gifts that will help me help others. I thank You Lord, the gifts You give are good and perfect. (Matthew 7:11; James 1:17.)

Because You are good, You will ensure all things will work together, for my good. You will cause everything, yes everything—even trials and difficult events—You will cause everything to work out for my benefit. (Romans 8:28.)

When God shows mercy to people, He bestows upon them kindness, beauty and steadfast love, He is being generous to us. God's blessings cannot be earned nor deserved, but He chooses to bless us according to His love.

I thank You Lord God—You are merciful and gracious, longsuffering and abundant in goodness and truth. You will be merciful to me forgiving my iniquity, transgression and sin. (Exodus 34:6-7.)

I thank You God, that You are the Father of mercies and the God of all comfort. I thank You Lord that You delight in mercy, and because of Your great love for me You will be rich in mercy and forgive my sin. (Micah 7:18; 2 Corinthians 1:3; Ephesians 2:4.)

I thank You Lord, that You pursue me because You are merciful. You pursue me so You can bless me with Your kindness and love. You follow me so You can bless me according to Your generosity. Lord, I do praise and worship You.

Lord, I thank You that You pursue me with Your goodness and mercy so that You can help me when I find the going tough, and You will strengthen me in times of weakness. Lord, I thank You that You will give me grace and mercy in time of need. (Hebrews 4:16.)

I thank You Lord that Your goodness and mercy follow me and overtake me especially when I stray from the right path. Your goodness and mercy will bring me back into the right way. Your goodness leads me to repentance. Your mercy cleanses me from my sin. Together, they bring me back to You—they will lead me to the table that You have prepared for me—they will lead me into Your "Oasis of Love". (Micah 7:18; Romans 2:4.)

"All the days of my life" is linked with the phrase "forever" in "I will dwell in the house of the Lord forever". This verse emphasises the truth that every moment of every single day of my life God's goodness and mercy shall follow me. "All" means the whole, every one, everything, the entirety, and implies totality. "All the days of my life" means "all my life long"—it asserts continuance, as does the word "forever" at the end of the verse.

I thank You Lord that regardless of problems and difficulties, trails and hardships, Your goodness and mercy will always be following me. I thank You Lord that whatever needs I will have, I know that You will meet them; whatever difficulties I will face, I know that You will help me through them.

I thank You Lord that today, tomorrow, next week, next month, next year and all the days after that, Your goodness and mercy will be following me. I thank You Lord—that there never will be a day, or even a moment in that day when Your goodness and mercy would not be following me.

I thank You Lord that I need not worry about tomorrow, or the day after that, or the day after that, or the day after that, for they are already in Your hand. And I know that on every day in the future—all the days of my life, Your goodness and mercy shall follow me, catch me and overwhelm me with blessings. (Matthew 6:33-34.)

I thank You Jesus that You are the same yesterday, today and forever, and since You are good and merciful, Your goodness and mercy towards me will never change. They will always be there behind me, following me, pursuing me, overtaking me and enveloping me in the midst of Your love. (Hebrews 13:8.)

How wonderful is Your love. As I go through the valley of the shadow of death, You are with me, at my side, to comfort, strengthen and lead me. Mercy and goodness are following me, pursuing me so that they will catch me and overwhelm me with blessings. Lord, how great You are.

CHAPTER 11

TOGETHER—FOREVER

And I will dwell in the house of the Lord forever. (Psalm 23:6 NKJV.)

*Since God is infinite and eternal, it is impossible for God to dwell on earth,
it is impossible for the heavens to contain Him. Yet God chooses to dwell in
certain places on earth so that finite man could meet with Him. So the term
"House of the Lord" is used for the place that God dwells. This can refer to the
tabernacle, or the temple, or to the place where people met with God in prayer.
God is present where people meet together to worship Him, and is with an
individual when he seeks God alone. God also dwells in His people's own lives.
(2 Chronicles 6:18; Matthew 6:6; 18:20; 21:13; Galatians 2:20.)*

I thank You Lord that because You love me so much, You just want to
be with me all the days of my life. So You will lead me into Your "Oasis
of Love" where we shall be together, enjoying our fellowship with each
other.

Lord, You want to be with me so much that Your goodness and mercy
shall follow me; they shall pursue me until they overtake and overwhelm
me. You will always be good to me. You will continually bless me with
Your mercy. You will do everything and anything to ensure I will be with
You, every single day of my life.

Lord You are so wonderful to me. Because You are my Good Shepherd,
You will continually guide me. You will always comfort me. You will

incessantly protect me and look after me with Your tender care. You are so good to me that I just want to be with You every day of my life, even forever.

Lord, You are so marvellous—You are the restorer of my soul, the provider of all my needs, and Your anointing and blessing upon me is so great that my cup overflows. I know Your goodness, I am blessed with Your mercy, I am overwhelmed with Your love . . . my desire is to be with You, in Your presence, all the days of my life.

Lord, in Your presence is fullness of joy. It is a joy that is not imperfect, incomplete or partial, but a joy that is full, satisfying, and abundant. I thank You Lord that this joy is unspeakable, inexpressible, and full of glory. (Psalm 16:11; 1 Peter 1:8.)

I thank You Lord that in Your presence are pleasures forevermore. You constantly hold gifts in Your hand; Your hand is never empty; it is inexhaustibly full of these gifts. You give them to Your children so that they can have pleasure and joy that lasts forever. But the greatest pleasure I have is just to be alone with You. (Psalm 16:11; Matthew 7:11.)

I thank You Lord that there is no better thing than to enter into Your presence and to stay there. I will rejoice with the opportunity of coming into Your presence. I will go into Your presence with shouts of joy and songs of thanksgiving. (Psalm 42:4; 122:1.)

Lord, I love You so much that I want to be where You are. I will spend time with You, my Love. Your presence means so much to me. I hunger and thirst after You. It is not the joy I seek after, nor the blessing, nor the anointing, but it is You, Yourself. As the deer pants for the water, so my soul pants after You. Just to be in Your presence is life itself. (Psalm 42:1.)

Lord, I love You. You have done so much for me because You first loved me. You lavish so many blessings upon me. You, Jesus, my Good Shepherd, gave up Your life for me. I adore You, I love You, and I worship You. You are everything to me. You are my life, my love and my joy. I love the place where Your glory dwells, my heart throbs for Your presence. (John 10:10-11, 15; 1 John 4:19; Psalm 26:8.)

I love You Lord, for You have been so gracious and wonderful to me. There is just one thing I want You to help me to do, there is just one desire in my life—that I may dwell in Your presence all the days of my life, that I may be with You and see how marvellous and wonderful You are. (Psalm 27:4.)

Psalm 84 reveals the Psalmist's heart concerning his desire to be in the presence of God.

How lovely is your dwelling-place, O Lord Almighty! (Psalms 84:1 NIV.)

God's house is described as "lovely" or "amiable". It refers to something or someone that is beloved, well loved or greatly loved. (a) (b) It is a word of endearment.

O Lord Almighty, I love You. The place where You dwell is a place of love, it is a place where lovers meet and I just want to be there with You. It is the centre of my life, because You dwell there. There is nowhere else that I desire to be. (Psalm 84:1.)

My soul longs, yes, even faints For the courts of the Lord; My heart and my flesh cry out for the living God. (Psalm 84:2 NKJV.)

Lord, I love You. I am so much in love with You that I have an intense desire to be in Your presence. I pine after You. I crave for You. My soul yearns for You so much that I faint for You. My entire body cries out for You. With my whole body, soul, strength and mind I desire You. All the longing of my heart are for You and You alone. I am besotted for You. My whole being just wants an intense and intimate communion and relationship with You. (Psalm 84:2.)

Blessed are those who dwell in your house; they are ever praising you. (Psalms 84:4 NIV.)

Lord, I love You. In Your presence, I am so blessed, happy and content that I will forever be praising You. There is nothing that can stop me from praising You. I will praise and worship You constantly and continually for I am in Your presence, You are the One I love. (Psalm 84:4.)

For a day in Your courts is better than a thousand. I would rather be a doorkeeper in the house of my God Than dwell in the tents of wickedness. (Psalm 84:10 NKJV.)

Lord, I love You. I love You so much that to spend a day in Your presence is by far a lot better than spending a thousand days elsewhere. Lord, I love You so much that to be with You is the desire of my heart—I don't want to be anywhere else. (Psalm 84:10.)

Lord, You love me so much that You want me to be with You all the days of my life. And if I do not come to You and spend time with You, You will come to the door of my heart and knock. And when I hear You and open wide the door of my heart to You, You will come in, You will have fellowship with me, and I will have fellowship with You. (Revelation 3:20.)

Lord, I love You so much that I want to be with You forever. For every single day, for the rest of my life, we will be with each other, loving each other and enjoying ourselves together. (Psalm 23:6.)

Lord. There will be one day when You will call me home, to be in Your presence forever and ever. And in heaven I will be with You and I will gaze upon Your wonderful face and I will fall down before You and worship You. Then, I will be living with You, and You will be living with me. And we shall be together, forever, throughout all eternity. Lord, I do look forward to that day. (John 14:3; Revelation 21:3; 22:4; 1 John 3:2.)

CHAPTER 12

I LOVE YOU LORD

God testified that David was "a man after my own heart". (Acts 13:22.) The proof of this was that he had not failed to keep any of God's commands—except concerning Bathsheba and her husband Uriah. (1 Kings 15:3-5; 2 Samuel 11:4, 15-17; 12:9-10.) But even in this, he repented, the prayer of which can be found in Psalm 51. In this Psalm, David mentions things that help us realise that he is a man after God's own heart, some of which are:

David knew that God wanted him to have honesty in his heart and life. (Psalm 51:6.)
David knew that God wanted him to have a pure and clean heart. (Psalm 51:10.)
David wanted to know the presence of God. (Psalm 51:11.)
David desired the fellowship of the Holy Spirit. (Psalm 51:11.)

Deep down in His heart, David loved God, David loved to be with God, and David loved having fellowship with the Holy Spirit. He didn't want anything to come between God and himself. He wanted to please God in all of his life so that he would have an intimate fellowship with God.

Let us take the journey into the love of God.

Search my heart Lord.

Lord, my heart is deceitful above all things, and desperately wicked. I cannot know my own heart. It conceals my true motives and intentions. I do not know if the reasons why I do things are pure or not. I don't know if my purposes are pleasing to You or not. Help me Lord, search my heart and test my mind. (Jeremiah 17:9-10.)

Search me, O God, and know my heart; try me, and know my thoughts. I really do want to please You in all things. Show me if there is any wicked way in me, and lead me in ways that are pleasing to You. (Psalm 139:23-24.)

How would you answer each question if Jesus were to say to you—

Do you love me more than anything or anyone else?
Do you love me?
Do you really love me?
Do you really love me, tenderly, passionately and intimately? (John 21:15-17.)

I will praise You Lord for Your love to me.

Looking at the love of God in some of the chapters in this book.

Lord, You are my Shepherd. You always hold me close to Your heart. You will never forget me. You will never forsake me. You are always with me, caring for me, holding me, guiding me, answering all of my prayers, so I can say "I shall not want".

Lord, You lead me into Your "Oasis of Love" where I will be safe and secure with You. You give me satisfaction as I lay down in the green pastures. You will give me refreshment beside the still waters. You will restore my soul, giving me strength in times of weakness, comfort in times of mourning, peace in times of anxiety and joy in times of testing. And You will make me rest content in Your presence, as we enjoy each other's fellowship.

Lord, You will always tenderly lead me in the way that You want me to go—in the way that is best for me. You will guide me along paths of righteousness—paths of rich blessing, where my joy will be complete, my peace will be perfect, and I will be filled with Your love.

And You will always lead me. There will never be a moment when You do not guide me. And when I walk through the valley of the shadow of death, You will still be with me, guiding, comforting, protecting and keeping me. And I will fear no evil because I know that You are at my side.

And You will lead me out of that dark valley, and bring me to a magnificent banquet that You have already prepared for me. There we will eat in fellowship together, and You will anoint my head with oil, pouring out upon me without measure Your Holy Spirit, Your love, Your joy . . .

And, every day of my life, Your goodness and mercy will always follow me, they shall catch me up and overtake me, they shall completely overwhelm me, so that I will dwell in Your loving presence, and we will be together, forever and ever, enjoying a beautiful intimate relationship.

I thank You Lord that I am so precious to You; I am Your treasured possession; I am the apple of Your eye; so Your love for me is caring and tender and Your protection of me is intense and passionate. You love me so much that You take delight in me; You rejoice over me; You will exult over me with loud singing. (Isaiah 43:4; 62:4-5; Deuteronomy 14:2; 32:10; Zephaniah 3:17.)

I praise You Lord that I am so beautiful in Your sight that I am like a crown of glory in Your hand. Indeed Lord, You see me as exceedingly beautiful that I am like a crown of royalty in Your hand. You see me as sparkling like jewels in Your crown.
(Isaiah 62:3; Zechariah 9:16.)

You love me so much Jesus, that as my Good Shepherd, You gave Your life for me; You died on the cross so I could receive forgiveness of my sins, and be accepted into Your Family as a child of God. I love You Jesus, because of Your amazing love for me.

I will respond to Your love, Lord.

Lord, I acknowledge that Your love is a "Love so amazing, so divine", and that it "demands my soul, my life, my all". [c] Lord, I know that You want me to love You with all of my heart, with all of my soul, with all of my mind and with all of my strength. (Mark 12:30.)

Lord, I know that You want me to love You affectionately, fervently, intimately, passionately, devotedly and tenderly. Lord, I know that You want me to love You more than anything else and more than anyone else. (John 21:15.)

I confess Lord.

Lord, I do not really love You as I ought. Lord, I do not spend enough time with You as I should. Lord, You are not in the centre of my life, nor on the throne of my heart.

Nevertheless I have this against you, that you have left your first love. Remember therefore from where you have fallen; repent . . . (Revelation 2:4-5 NKJV.)

I thank You Lord that even though I have forsaken my first love, You have not forsaken me. I thank You Lord that even though I have abandoned the love I had at first for You, You have not abandoned me.

Lord, this place of love is the highest place in my life that I can have with You. Lord, being deeply in love with You is the most important thing of my life. I thank You Lord that I can repent and turn back to You. I know that You will forgive me and restore me.

I know your works, that you are neither cold nor hot. I could wish you were cold or hot. So then, because you are lukewarm, and neither cold nor hot, I will vomit you out of My mouth. As many as I love, I rebuke and chasten. Therefore be zealous and repent. Behold, I stand at the door and knock. If anyone hears My voice and opens the door, I will come in to him and dine with him, and he with Me. (Revelation 3:15-16, 19-20 NKJV.)

Lord, I admit that I am neither hot nor cold in my love for You. Lord, I confess that I am lukewarm towards You. I thank You Lord that You have not given up on me.

I thank You Lord that You are knocking at my heart's door, asking if I would allow You to come back into the centre of my life. I thank You

Lord that as I am enthusiastic and zealous in repenting, as I ask You back into the centre of my heart and life, then You will come in, forgive me and allow that intimate relationship to be restored.

Lord, I receive Your forgiveness.

I thank You Lord that as I admit that I have sinned by leaving my first love, and confess my sins, You are faithful and just and You will forgive my sins and cleanse me from all things that are not pleasing to You. (1 John 1:9.)

I thank You Lord, that when I confess and turn from my sin, You forgive me and will remember my sin no more. You will take my sins from me and cast them behind Your back where You will see them no more. You will tread my sins underfoot and hurl them into the depths of the sea, where they will be lost forever. (Jeremiah 31:34; Isaiah 38:17; Micah 7:18-19.)

Lord, I will love You every day of my life.

Lord, to know You in a more deeper and intimate way is the most important thing for me to do in my life. Lord, I will consider everything else as rubbish that I may win You and develop a loving relationship with You. (Philippians 3:8-10.)

Lord, You know all things. You know I love You. Please help me to love You more and to express my love to You in ways that are pleasing to You.

1. Lord, I will spend time in Your presence

   Lord, I want to spend more time on my own with You, in worship and prayer.

   Lord, I thank You that You are my Good Shepherd. There is one thing I want more than anything else—that is to spend time in Your presence every day that I may gaze upon Your beauty. (Psalm 27:4.)

   Lord, help me to come into the closet, and close the door on all things that I may spend time alone with You. Free from all distractions and ignoring all interruptions, I just want to spend time with You. (Matthew 6:6.)

2. Lord, I will do Your will

Lord, help me to reveal my love to You by doing those things that You have asked and taught me to do. As I show my love for You, Jesus, You and the Father will love me and You both will come to me and make Your home with me. (John 14:15, 21, 23.)

Lord, help me to remain in Your love by keeping Your commandments, then Your joy will be in me and my joy will be complete and overflowing. (John 15:9-11.)

3. Lord, I will be continually filled with Your Spirit

Lord, fill me and continue to fill me with Your Holy Spirit that I may know and practically experience the breadth and length and height and depth of Your love, which far surpasses mere knowledge. Lord so fill me with Your Holy Spirit and love, that I may be filled and flooded through my whole being with the richest measure of Your presence, O God. (Ephesians 3:18-19.)

Lord, continue to fill me with Your Holy Spirit. Pour out Your love into my heart through Your Holy Spirit. Fill me so much with Your love that it will gush out of me, so that I will love You more and more and more and more. And I know that this love will also pour out from me to others. (Romans 5:5; John 7:37-38.)

Lord, I love You

Lord, You know all things.
You know that I love You.
You know that I really do love You.
You know that I really do love You, tenderly, passionately and intimately.

I love You Lord. You are my beloved. I belong to You. (Song 2:16; 6:3.)

Reference Works

(a) From the Complete Word Study Dictionary, Old Testament, by Warren Baker, D.R.E. and Eugene Carpenter, Ph.D. Copyright © 2003 by AMG Publishers. All rights reserved.

(b) From the Theological Wordbook of the Old Testament. Copyright © 1980 by The Moody Bible Institute of Chicago. All rights reserved.

(c) From "When I survey the wondrous cross" by Isaac Watts.

(d) From More Perfect Illustrations for Every Topic and Occasion. Copyright © 2002 by Craig Brian Larson & Drew Zahn. English US edition © 2004 by Biblesoft with permission of Tyndale House Publishers, Inc. All rights reserved.

(e) From Perfect Illustrations for Every Topic and Occasion. Copyright © 2002 by Craig Brian Larson & Drew Zahn. English US edition © 2004 by Biblesoft with permission of Tyndale House Publishers, Inc. All rights reserved.